un**K**onditional

Boundless Acceptance of a Beautiful Chaotic Soul

ADRIA DEVAUGHNS

Printed in the United States of America
First Printing 2021
First Edition 2021

ISBN: 978-1-955393-89-8

10 9 8 7 6 5 4 3 2 1

Iqra Publishing Inc. books may be purchased for inspiration, business, education, or sale promotions use. For information please email iqrapublishing@gmail.com

Published & Distributed by:
Iqra Publishing Inc.
157 Sunset Avenue NW, Atlanta, GA 30331
http://iqrapublishing.com
Edited by Editor in Chief: Victor Trionfo of the IPI team.

Iqra Publishing Inc

Love yourself so that you can love others
so that others can love you as you love yourself.

Dedication

I dedicate this book to my failures and successes for it is the combination of them all that make me the person I am today. To those that genuinely love and support me it is my hope that I have loved you more thru my actions and not just my words.

To my readers you are a beautiful expression of the creator. It is my hope to empower you thru my words to see yourself more clearly thru the faded reflection that stares back at you from your mirror.

For it is the culmination of the light and the dark that makes me the complex individual that stands before you.

Table of Contents

un*K*onditional PREFACE

I didn't want to write this book, rather I had to write this book. It's just the responsible thing to do. I've spent the bulk of my life sidestepping internal turbulence much like yourself, perhaps. So, call this my un*K*onditional contribution to society where the "*K*" represents *K*arma. I make the case for grace, humility, tolerance, self love, mastering your emotional IQ, vibrating out high frequencies of positivity, and smart resource utilisation and risk management to becoming God's intention of you.

You were not meant to be 1/10th or even one half of you any more than you were meant to be a cow. If you look into the mirror of your soul, and you see you withering away, then this book is for you. Chances are, you've given away too much of you to others and too little to you and your Creator and have given attention to almost none of the Universal Laws of existence. Maybe you were or are oppressed, stressed, or traumatized on some level and fighting for your life without proper healing tools. I just feel that if I knew then what I know now, my life would have attracted more abundance, not just physically, but mentally and emotionally. It's highly likely that this will apply to you as well. The target of this work is to get you to be the best you, the most complete and clear reflection of you, the most successful you, the best "other half" of the relationship, the most abundant you, achieving your highest potential, your Highest Good. But why do I feel compelled to share my story and my angle on life with you?

It's simple. I care. I'm a softie and I care about the struggles of humanity. I experienced trauma as a child, and given the nature of the loss which triggered my traumatic experience, I was unable to recover according to relationships I engaged in from my early adulthood until this very day. I lost someone extremely close to me, and as a child of my social status, I wasn't offered the opportunity to process that emotion properly. And so, here I am with a very compelling story that should encourage those of you who are experiencing the same, or perhaps, you know someone close to you that you may be responsible for or even responsible for causing the trauma, to seek proper counsel and therapy to coach the victim, be it you, a loved one, or friend, to calmer waters.

Personally, my life had multiple stages of manifestation of trauma, and you find that, at some point, I was totally oblivious to a condition such as Post Traumatic Stress Disorder (PTSD). Funny thing about inadvertent denial, those teen and early adult years were pretty normal for me, or so it seemed. It was when I grew older and attempted to formulate normal, healthy relationships that I began experiencing the invisible. Trauma has no face, gender, age, or racial preference. Sure, there are reported statistics which may point to a race of people who seem to have experienced an undue share of traumatic experiences, but that's due to other factors influencing the activation of trauma. I'm speaking to everyone, even those intentionally responsible for being the main ingredient or seed of trauma for the victim. Love is not a characteristic of induced trauma, which may last a lifetime for the undeserving and unsuspecting victim. Hatred, no matter how you color it, is still hatred, so since you know the potential of expressed hatred, why not turn the table, spin the board and really place yourself in that person's seat, walk a mile in their shoes, and try to feel damaging emotions and stress they are experiencing. Take a look in the mirror, analyze the clarity or cloudiness of the reflection, make a change or an appropriate decision protecting the wellbeing of another. Likewise, uncontrollable events are what they are, so an unfortunate circumstance which plants the seed of trauma may be unavoidable, but the aftershock and effect can and should be managed to cure or curb trauma's appetite for lasting effects.

With all that has been going on with me internally, trying to heal the wounds of my past, the wounds of our people continue to be inflicted upon us. The chaos that abounds in society right now is unreal and difficult to digest. For years we have watched our men, who pose no serious threat, slain in the streets, and, naturally, we all go into a fit of rage for about a week or three, and then it is back to business as usual. We are more than a hashtag, yet there are some who continue to diminish our existence to just that, and it's sad to watch, hard to swallow. But what about family dejecting family, diminishing blood relatives' existence to ghost-like presence? I'll tell you all about that.

It's disheartening to witness the maleficent treatment black and brown people have endured at the hands of civilians and authorities who refuse to see and acknowledge that their lives really do have worth and meaning. And to be clear, I make absolutely no distinction in black on black crime in our major cities at alarming, horrifying and disgustingly shameful rates statistically versus racially fueled acts of fiery hatred and dismissal of human quality, equality, and reverence for life. It is hurtful and mind numbing to watch black men savagely slain or any decent human being for that matter, but this is more of a black matter. Somehow, they and we as well have been conditioned to believe that we are inferior and expendable. I just wish we could think reverently about ourselves and have others think the same about us as a people and individually.

Our skin color or the texture of our hair, or the street address, or apartment complex, or housing we live in, makes us no less deserving of respect in its most genuine form. There are enough resources for us all to live in harmony, and this we will learn from the Law of Abundance. The inhumane, irreverent disregard for the lives of black men in today's day is hardly fathomable, and, equally, that genocidal tendency and insensitive nature of our black men is intensely alarming. I want you to know that I honor you, and your life matters. But we must gain something from this book even if it's only one pivotal point, life matters first and foremost within — love, respect and honor begins with us, and I address that with self love. Perhaps many of you inflicting trauma are traumatized yourselves. That's covered as well. This book can give you pause to think about the current path of resistance and destruction that you are on even if it's self destruction. Healing is possible no matter where you are on your tare of terror. Whether you are a menace to society in the eyes of authority or those you terrorize, completely healed, or completely wounded, you have worth and meaning inherently within.

To have experienced being treated as if my existence meant nothing gives me an interesting pause, but I have learned to accept that that is the culprit's issue, and my skin color is not a definition of character or integrity. If someone chooses to judge me because of my skin and not the content of my character, then the problem lies within them. I have experienced subtle displays of disregard simply predicated on my appearance, racially. Something as simple as a greeting was unafforded me because of the faint hue of my skin, albeit quite light in complexion. But because it is not as light as others, I was deemed unworthy of such a simple gesture of kindness. How much more dissatisfying than when this snub comes from within your own circle. Yeah, I've had to deal with that as a direct result of my loss, and it's an indescribable feeling of being shunned by those who should be thicker than water because they are your blood, yet they flow clear as in void of familial love and acceptance.

But through it all, I gravitate towards the center, and there I find peace. I focus on the bright spots embellished by the warmth and light of the sun and the brilliance of today's horizon. Speaking of which, I am elated to see the power of women of color stroke the canvas of "la Casa Blanco" as they paint the forefront with vibrant color whether others choose to accept it or not. Considering the last couple of years, I am bothered by the way women of color have been portrayed in the media, and I'm not even sure if it were intentionally "art•chestrated" or just a slip of ignorance with casual, inartful brush strokes. We are, in my estimation, portrayed in a very negative light at every convenient opportunity, certainly not the portrait of flattery hoped for and welcomed by a people of struggle and virtuosity. However, it is refreshingly inspiring to see the power and tenacity of women of color surface and surge to take their posts.

It is amazing to see strong women standing boldly in their power, fighting for that which is just and kind for the wellbeing of all mankind. They are sterling, striving at the pinnacle of their highest good and standing in this power to ensure that our people are afforded equal opportunity. And why not, given that opportunity has been on the table for the majority for centuries? I mean not to exclude, so I approach this not in a manner of deprivation of others but in a way that is all inclusive. We can deal with the mind games that people play to keep us in a state of confusion and anxiety, but it is quite another thing of intentional acts of those who hold some preconceived notion of a threat regarding one's intelligence or even existence. With a gushing exhale, a refreshing, gentle, cool current whisks around the corner and down the corridors of government to tease the locks of women who look like me, striking a pose, historically posted in previously verboten positions of leadership for us. Gratefully, it gives us all long deferred gratification, and as for me, hope that I too can achieve greatness by standing in my own power while overcoming the odds, allowing my light to shine on those who can see and feel my genuine concern for the well-being of those whom grace my presence as well as those who are distantly near to my heart.

These extraordinarily gifted women stand in the gap to boldly effect positive change specifically for people of color as well as the whole. They are unbiased in their pursuit of what is right and just for every person, and I am honored to witness such greatness in these women of integrity and grace in a time like this. They all bring their unique flavor, accentuating justice, teasing, agitating, and exciting the palate of government with tastefulness.

Madame Vice President Kamala Harris gives us long awaited history as she graces the highest position in government ever held by a female, not to mention her ethnicity. And as for me, through her smile alone, hope and happiness envelopes me with warmth and radiance. An historic victory, an election for the ages, a proud followup moment for suffragettes, I am overjoyed that a nation divided chose this age to come together so overwhelmingly, uplifting nations around the globe with acknowledgment of worth and trust in the intelligence of a woman while cognizant of her heritage.

Amanda Gorman, an adorable sweetheart; she gives me poise, she gives me prose, she sends chills of innocent and conscious creativity through my cranium, irradiating through my spine. She is reminiscent of those ignited by righteous fuel of equity to stoke the pilot flame in eager, intelligent young people insisting on changing the tapestry of world government and wealth one stitch, one seam, one embroidered and crafted word at a time.

Mayor Kesha Lance Bottoms gives me a spirit of nurture. She stood on the podium and urged "The City," ATLiens, to go home and not resort to violence. The power of a loving mother urging her children to be peaceful, wow! I was compelled to drive to the scene of demonstration that next morning after Rashard Brooks was killed. The energy was so intense rolling down the offramp as I exited the interstate. The air was filled with rage and pain. It moved me to tears, which is not too hard to do anyway, but still. It made the hair on my arms stand up. There were people walking around cleaning up, and you could sense their somber mood. I do not know why I was compelled to be in that space and could not make sense of it. I tried being open about it, but my effort was only met with queries of my character and faith.

Two term former First Lady Michelle Obama gives me sophistication, earthiness, and nurturing as well. She exudes unKonditional class, grace, heart, realness and sensibility. I am in awe of her insatiability for the welfare of the people of this nation and mankind in general as well as her ability to stay grounded despite grand notoriety. Intelligent and averse to nonsense, she brought style and ethereal overtone to the highest office, and with an emotional outcry for what is right for our people, she moved a nation to save itself from self destruction.

Stacy Abrams emits a fighting spirit unKonditionally, and I am enticed to fight right alongside her. Do not get me wrong, she's very much graceful, but she has that fury, that fight spirit within her so enormous that no one can tame. She resembles the epitome of "get knocked down – get back up." She shows true heart, illustrative of "the how to" of getting back up and fighting even smarter another day. Her fight in the trenches to register voters parallels the suffragan's stride, and her future, as she sails through rough political waters, will be guided by a bright beacon beckoning her ship and anchor at the lighthouse perched atop the cliff on the shore of Capitol Hill.

Prov 8 [1]Does not wisdom cry out, And understanding lift her voice? [2]She takes her stand on the top of the high hill ... [10]Receive my instruction, and not silver, And knowledge rather than choice gold; [11]For wisdom is better than rubies, and all the things one may desire cannot be compared with her. (NKJV)

These unique and extraordinary women of wisdom bring something palatable to the table, and they shine their light unfiltered, effecting positive change internally and externally for those magnetized, drawn near to their words and brave, novel actions. Like these women, you too can find you, find your most incredible you. I weave in and out with wicker of despair mitigated by hope and encouragement crafting my case for the greatest you by making sound arguments ranging from creation to artificial intelligence and nanotechnology in medicines and vaccines this very day. I take you on a futuristic ride with The Jetsons™ to healthier relationships. You will be introduced to genius prior to and as of our time to make the point of comparison between IQ and Emotional IQ. Increase and wellness to the enrichment of your life taps into the Universal Laws, our Monotheistic religions, and philosophy of the ages.

So this is what I'm not: I'm not a professional Counselor, Therapist, Physicist, Biologist, Chemist, Medical Doctor or Doctor of any kind. I am Adria, a modest champion of love in its purest form and a vessel of enlightenment to usher as many as I can into the tunnel of light leading to the realm of personal Highest Good. That which I share with you is universal and applicable to my life, and my hope is that my experiences and the Universal Laws will be adopted with an adaptation to your situation and life in general.

Well then, there's who I am not and who I am. This sums up my view on our interconnected spirits and my wish for all humanity

"Though I am a unique individual, I am not an individual with a unique set of circumstances, rather an individual with a "You!nique" set of circumstances, for I am "You!niversal," I am You! The Highest Good of each individual would undoubtedly transcend societal norms which cause us to hate or not dole out love to those truly worthy or simply in need. But we could start with just you, and a new societal norm could ride a tidal wave, creating an exponential curve of tolerance infused with universal love and acceptance for the Greater Good of all. Instead of succumbing to a virus, let our Highest Good ascend, soaring to viral stratum."[1]

Victor Trionfo, 2021

---

[1] Trionfo, Victor (Alias), 2021, Editor in Chief.

1 unKonditional SELF

The power of self now is run by the fossil fuel of history and the desired outcome of the future.

i. Mirror of Faded Reflection

I encourage you to read the preface unconditionally prior to looking into the mirror of faded reflection. Kudos, if you already have. The hardest place in the world to look is in the mirror. Looking in the mirror takes a level of courage and commitment that most may not be willing to explore. It is easier to emphasize fault in others because the faded reflection in the mirror reveals truths that one may not have the courage to face. In fact, facing any level of truth about self can sometimes prove too difficult given the depth of discovery the faded reflection might reveal. None of us are able to look at our mirror image and render to ourselves the rawest truth. Why is that?

Why are we not able to be honest with and about self first? Studies may show that we are capable of things that we do not want to admit to. If we are timid and insecure, we may not want to own that faded reflection's fact-finding. It's the "this can't be me" syndrome. Limitations scare us, quite frankly. And flaws beamed back at us give us a guilt complex. Look too hard, and you may see shattered dreams that appear too monumental for your character, charisma, current means, and your current reality. Maybe that's why, but one must acknowledge the rifts in their own personality to reach any level of self-sovereignty and freedom. It will not always be easy to see and admit one's own flaws, but doing so will create space for one to see the truth of how they show up in relationships and assess if their ways of being and thinking serve the greater good of every person involved. It also gives change for one to account for their own active participation in the rise and fall of relationships around them.

Accounting for one's own behavior, good, bad, or indifferent, opens the door to unlearn old thought processes and learn more effective ways of being that will foster attitudes of peace and harmony. It is time to discontinue playing the blame game with other people, thus creating space for self-accountability. Not only should we hold others accountable, but it is imperative that we also hold ourselves accountable for our actions or inaction. We must even hold ourselves accountable for the decisions we make allowing the lack of morality incessant in others to become the norm in our existence. Self-reflection of those truths requires deeper examination of the root cause of pain that manifests in the person staring back from the faded reflection in the mirror.

Becoming whole is a process of peeling back the layers of broken promises, dreaming against the odds, disappointments, setbacks, failures, unrequited love, and even the narratives created by conditioned belief that one repeatedly tells themselves.

The best way to peel back each of those layers is to first introduce a small incision of authority to give oneself the permission to acknowledge one's feelings, embrace what we feel, then gently lift that layer for deeper introspection. Somewhere along the way, we have become afraid to genuinely "feel our feelings," and that's if we allow ourselves to feel at all. We have become so accustomed to putting on the façade of a brave front that we never exercise our own ability to express our vulnerability to others and worse, not even to ourselves.

When a person acknowledges their feelings, they must ask themselves, "Self, why do these feelings exist?" Understanding why they exist facilitates the journey to finding the true source of one's pain. People have given their hearts time and time again, only to have them rejected, thrown back over and over repeatedly. It is understandable that this thing of perpetual rejection takes a toll on the feeble, but also on the strongest at heart.

That faded reflection in the mirror is tired, worn out, wounded and dejected. It is plausible that all people want is to repossess the pieces of themselves they needlessly give away. That is a path back to wholeness, a reclaiming of oneself. Taking back the power of self, and standing fully in the truth of that power is true wholeness. Once a person looks in the mirror, they must acknowledge the unprocessed truth of who they have become, then remain objective to those moments of indifference that the person in the reflection had to face. The journey home to self is not for the faint at heart, but it is a beautiful journey nonetheless. It is not at all easy to unlearn years of conditioned thinking, but unconditional in the sense that one must re-evaluate those things that take away from or add value to one's life. I had to ask myself, "Do I believe these things because I believe them, or do I believe this because somebody told me to?"

ii. Jettisoning

On the road to becoming a better you, I introduce the concept of jettisoning because it is key to the journey of reaching the Highest Good of the individual, and that requires dead level focus. To jettison is to eliminate or release those people, places, things, and beliefs that no longer serve forward progression of the wellness of the individual, holistically. Even the Jetsons™ were jettisoned as futuristic as they were. But Hanna-Barbera was living in the moment and the moment wasn't living up to the vivid creation of the colorful Jetsons™. In fact, the Jetsons™ had no color at all for more than 97% of viewers as only less than three percent of all households had color televisions and even fewer could view this futuristic cartoon in its brilliant color being syndicated for only 24 episodes in 1962 - 1963.

Because of the nature of the color palette, the black and white rendering was not as alluring as Hanna-Barbera wanted, and so they jettisoned the Jetsons™ even projecting space age technology with Googie styled architecture and a smarthome with robots and a lifestyle set in the year 2062. We are still yearning for the personal flying machine, etc., today! But the Jetsons had a problem of being ahead of its time and consequently no longer benefited the immediate progression of the company.

But there's a lesson here to be learned other than people, places, and things not fitting in. Not only was Hanna-Barbera brilliant, but shortsighted as well. As hugely successful as they were with some 120 cartoons, movies and sitcoms, they didn't have the foresight of even what they were projecting ahead of its time; cloud commuting, cloud computing, business cloud to cloud, and personal remote storage minus the Jetsons™ physically whisking off to work from cloud to cloud. But then again, they weren't a hi-tech conglomerate and therefore it wasn't there focus. They focused on what they were superior at, funny cartoons, and the color television soon caught up to their portfolio. Their dynasty took on an even more colorful repertoire and while the Jetsons™ no longer fit into their money-making portfolio and progressive social strategy, they were reintroduced for 51 episodes from 1985-87. But now you understand why the Jetsons™ were canceled, jettisoned.

Understanding the "why" behind decisions made facilitates the journey to finding inner peace and releases the karmic debris of cultural and social conditioning acted out in each decision. This journey is a re-evaluation about what fits with whom one is currently and what will fit in that person's life for the foreseeable future in the moments to come. Seeing things as they are and not as we wish them to be will eliminate undue stress and heartache, but vision must not be forsaken.

This requires a willingness to make the hard decisions in the moment when it comes to peace of self, relationships, faith, and love of life, thereby honoring the things that are of utmost importance real-time, and as a visionary, the future.

iii. Focus Quadrants - God's & Technology Perspective

Real time perspective steers focus to the present moment, which is of great importance in life. And the present moment should be considered with a broader perspective than what is available to you just for the immediate moment, but rather what's on the horizon and within reach. It serves immeasurable purpose to evaluate where one is in the present with extreme focus while tapping into the database of history, the past, to study and evaluate the outcome of actions or inaction so that you may carve out a clear path to your desired destination well into the future.

This is a very intricate concept, and I fear that a cursory glance at the bold, short bursts here may miss the mark if I don't cautiously emphasize that the past ignored sets one up for repeating history, good or bad, inadvertently. Likewise, regarding the absence of future focus says to discard planning, and we know that failing to plan for the future is a setup in that we plan to fail. So, while we pin focus to the walls of present, we do so with respect to the experiences of yesterday and tactical and strategic planning of goals for the future with near-term visibility of what's soon to be available to us.

I strongly feel that since faith is a necessary attribute for my target audience and subject matter that the creator be given some stage time, but let's consider this first:

Focus for the individual can be apportioned into 4 quadrants, the past, the present, the desirable future, and the unknown tangentially.

The power of self now is run by the fossil fuel of history and the desired outcome of the future. While we should not dwell on the past, we should certainly learn from it, equipping our toolbox of life with valuable instruments used for a more promising future of avoidance or inclusion. And while acting now satisfies the actuate component of our focus, the planning quadrant of our desirable future cannot be left untouched, invisible or not visited. While the unknown can be daunting — scarier than you can imagine even — we must plan our desires with that in mind simultaneously. The fear of the unknown can be crippling without a viable support structure, vision, and plan of contingency, alternatives and a strong foundation in faith.

Consider, philosophically, the will of God. According to Dr. Garry Friesen, a well known author and evangelist, we should consider the individual will of God (the Dot) encircled by the Moral Will, which is encircled by the Sovereign Will of God to determine the plan for one's life.

Without delving too deeply into such a philosophy, I use this as an example of God's plan for the individual. The will of God is all about a plan for the individual's future. Incidentally, this concept does not necessarily support the "Dot" theological concept of God's pinpointed or specific will for the individual, rather leans more toward the Moral Will for all individuals which presents many options for us within blessed attributes, talent and moral specification. "We know that God orchestrates history to work all things for the good of those who are called according to His purpose. All things will end with God, and we can trust that He is keeping us in His consideration. We are to follow His moral law, not pray we hit the 'dot' and live and perform the exact actions God wants us to."[2]

---

[2] Friesen, Garry, ThM, ThD and Maxson, J. Robin, ThM, Decision Making and the Will of God: A Biblical Alternative to the Traditional View, revised Edition

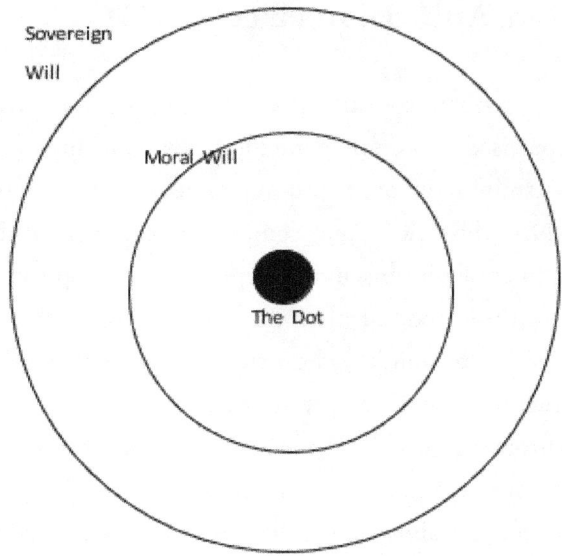

WILL OF GOD

a. Artificial Intelligence (AI)

Further, consider Artificial Intelligence (AI), an advanced human supervised computer method of learning patterned behavior for determining or predicting outcomes based on Artificial Neural Networks (ANN), historical data, complex Evolving Algorithms (EA's), and a large number of neurons and perceptrons. A perceptron is a binary classification algorithm modeled after the functioning of the human brain — it was intended to emulate the neuron. The perceptron, while it has a simple structure, has the ability to learn and solve very complex problems. Each neuron can make simple decisions and feeds those decisions to other neurons organized in interconnected layers. Together, the neural network can emulate almost any function and answer practically any question, given enough training samples and computing power. A "shallow" neural network has only three layers of neurons.

A Deep Neural Network (DNN) has a similar structure, but it has two or more "hidden layers" of neurons that process inputs. Deep learning networks are more accurate than shallow neural networks and improve in accuracy as more neuron layers are added. [But even neural networks have boundaries.] Additional layers are useful up to a limit of 9-10, after which their predictive power starts to decline. [That means that in our relationships, we too can get to points of diminishing returns.] Today most neural network models and implementations use a deep network of between 3-10 neuron layers.[3]

How does it work? Getting straight to the point, AI using neurons or nodes emulating human neurons and perceptrons as well as human

---

[3] Neural Network Concepts, The Complete Guide to Artificial Neural Networks: Concepts and Models,
https://missinglink.ai/guides/neural-network-concepts/complete-guide-artificial-neural-netw orks/

intelligence doesn't focus on the here and the now. Rather, it focuses on the future by learning from as many data points of the past as are available, outliers included, and patterns which are closely tested and adjusted during the training phase by human engineering performing tasks that are viewed as impossible by the naked human brain. Yet, controlling the modeling and evolving the models is an intense process requiring human input. The more data points available, the more learned and effective AI combined with EA's becomes in predicting the future, thereby aiding us in bridging the gap between the known from experience to the feared unknown. With Covid-19, every algorithm known to man and now other neural networks of neurons or nodes are being employed to compete against each other to be able to predict the outcome of the future, given the many variables and unknowns. AI is now being combined with nanotechnology to make even more effective application in nanomedicine. That is the essence of AI. And that essence considers the past and the here and now as well as foreseeable or future resources, constantly evolving, increasing their probability of effectiveness to determine the degree of success in containing this deadly virus with CDC imposed guidelines as well as sophisticated nanotechnology, assuming that you believe and acknowledge that Covid-19 is a serious virus responsible for the deaths of millions.

b. Nanotechnology

Nanotechnology has been around for several decades. Well, centuries actually. We simply looked into the past and improved the technology looking forward to integrating it more closely with AI for greater target precision, predictions and application. But only now is it being unveiled on a world stage. It is the ability to study life-forms at a highly precise one billionth of a meter or 10^{-9} meters power of visibility, accuracy, and engineering specifically and especially in molecular biology with the study of molecules and atoms and engineered nanomachines to interact with the body's nano-world on a molecular nanoscale of one to 100 nanometers.

Just before the baby boomers, hippies, color TV, and the Jetsons™, another baby was born in 1959 as Physicist Richard Feynman became the Father of Nanotechnology, although the brainchild was not named as such at that time. It was in the heart of the disco era and the space age over a decade later, in his explorations of ultraprecision machining, Professor Norio Taniguchi, initials NT, coined the term NanoTechnology. But it wasn't until 1981, just a few years or so before the return of the Jetsons™ and the development of the scanning tunneling microscope (STM) enabling us to "see" individual atoms that modern nanotechnology was birthed. When you look at the brilliance and longevity today of paint used by the Egyptians on ancient artifacts some 5000 years ago, one could easily deduce that they applied nanotechnology with the process of engineering colors with gold and silver as well as ink from sea creatures. The same is true of stained glass art in medieval times.

Viruses are life-forms just as are humans. Intricate studies in chemistry and molecular biology have taught us so much about the human body that we have successfully introduced high-tech vaccines to medicine for the general public that directs your DNA through mRNA (messenger RNA) and spawns the natural production of antigens to fight COVID-19. We even know that if we string together the blood vessels of an average sized adult, the blood vessels will wrap around the earth 2.5 times. Because of studies from the past, we know that the human body has vesicles, tiny boats which ferry between docking stations to transport protein from the source to a specific target in the cell and extracellular environment. What we've learned from the past helps us in the present and prepares us for a more technologically advanced future in the world of the unknown. So in our focus, we study the engineering of the past and applied science to effect the science of today with our desires of future applications on an even grander scale.

The creator obviously dealt on a nanoscale in nanotechnology to design and create life and the universe to support life, so let's take a closer look at our molecular structure, beginning with a nucleic tutorial of sorts to support how vital the Focus Quadrant concept proposed is to life itself.

1) Nucleic Acid Overview

In molecular biology, we find fascinating molecules vital to the existence and perpetuation of life itself. There are four biomolecules considered the four "molecules of life" as listed: Nucleic acids, proteins, carbohydrates and lipids. The average human deals with proteins and carbs on a daily basis, but our bodies deal with all four every second of our lives.

Nucleic acids are long polymers made up of individual elements called nucleotides which individually consists of three elements of its own: one to three phosphate groups, a ribose sugar and one of four possible nitrogenous bases. A nucleotide is the monomeric unit of a nucleic acid. Nucleic acids are the only biomolecules that cannot be metabolized to generate adenosine triphosphate (ATP, the "energy currency" of cells).[4]

Adenosine is a nucleoside $C_{10}H_{13}N_5O_4$ that is a constituent of RNA and yields adenine and ribose on hydrolysis.[5]

---

[4] Beck, Kevin, DNA vs RNA: What are the Similarities & Differences? (with Diagram), Updated
April 23, 2019,
https://sciencing.com/dna-vs-rna-what-are-the-similarities-differences-with-diagram-13718421.html

[5] "Adenosine." Merriam-Webster.com Medical Dictionary, Merriam-Webster,
https://www.merriam-webster.com/medical/Adenosine. Accessed 3 Feb. 2021.

Adenine is a purine base $C_5H_5N_5$ that codes hereditary information in the genetic code in DNA and RNA.[6]

DNA (Deoxy-ribonucleic Acid), and RNA (ribonucleic acid) are the two nucleic acids found in nature, and these are our personality signature, the molecules which determine uniquely who we are. DNA and RNA both carry chemical information in the form of a nearly identical and logically straightforward genetic code. Simply put, DNA is the creator and the vehicle by which the message is relayed to successive generations of cells as well as complete organisms. RNA is the conveyor of the message from the foreman that gives instructions to the molecular assembly-line workers.[7]

Nature is the progenitor of synthesis, manufacturing, warehousing, logistics, and distribution; and this — this is manufacturing at its finest. Nothing new under the sun, says Solomon, the man of profound wisdom and riches. He was granted both by He who created the universe with "Wii" and a touch of Love. That's the original Wii controller, not a game controller, but God himself. Yes, it took Wisdom, information, intelligence and a touch of Love to create a universe designed to support life which supports the life of God's highest creation, humanity. You see this in Genesis 1-2 and richly in Proverbs as wisdom is apparent and the focus of each, and interestingly in Proverbs 8, specifically, we see Wisdom illustrated as a woman.

Prov 8 [1]Does not wisdom cry out, And understanding lift her voice? [2]She takes her stand on the top of the high hill … [10]Receive my instruction, and not

---

[6] "Adenine." Ibid.

[7] Beck, Kevin, DNA vs RNA: What are the Similarities & Differences? (with Diagram), Updated
April 23, 2019,
https://sciencing.com/dna-vs-rna-what-are-the-similarities-differences-with-diagram-13718421.html

silver, And knowledge rather than choice gold; [11]*For wisdom is better than rubies, and all the things one may desire cannot be compared with her. (NKJV)*

So now to continue with the tutorial of nucleic acid overview, I direct the focus to messenger RNA, the brightest star of medicine today and the foreseeable future.

DNA and RNA are codependent, and DNA is directly responsible for messenger ribonucleic acid (mRNA) synthesis in the process called transcription. Read by a ribosome in the process of synthesizing a protein, mRNA is a single-stranded molecule of RNA that corresponds to the genetic sequence of a gene. DNA also relies on RNA to carry out its function flawlessly and expeditiously to convey its instructions to ribosomes within the cells. The nucleic acids, DNA and RNA, have an interdependence qualifying both roles as equally vital to the mission of life.

DNA molecules are considerably longer than RNA molecules; in fact, a single DNA molecule makes up the genetic material of an entire chromosome, accounting for thousands of genes. Also, the fact that they are separated into chromosomes at all is a testament to their comparative mass. Although RNA has a more humble profile, it is actually the more diverse of the two molecules from a functional standpoint. In addition to coming in tRNA, mRNA and rRNA forms, RNA can also act as a catalyst (enhancer of reactions) in some situations, such as during protein translation.

The purpose of mRNA is to create a mobile, encoded set of directions for the synthesis of proteins. A length of DNA that includes the "blueprint" for a single protein product is called a gene. Each three-nucleotide sequence carries the instructions for making a particular amino acid, with amino acids being the building blocks of proteins in the same way nucleotides are the building blocks of nucleic acids. There are 20 amino acids in all, allowing for an essentially unlimited number of combinations and permutations, hence, protein products. When an mRNA molecule becomes attached to a translation site along the ribosome, it is joined by a particular kind of tRNA that carries a specific amino acid (there are therefore 20 different flavors of tRNA, one for each amino acid). This occurs because the tRNA can "read" the three-nucleotide sequence on the exposed mRNA that corresponds to a given amino acid. When the tRNA and mRNA "match up," the tRNA releases its amino acid, which is added to the end of the growing amino acid chain destined to become a protein. This polypeptide reaches its specified length when the mRNA molecule is read in its entirety, and the polypeptide is released and processed into a bonafide protein.

Transfer RNA (tRNA) is a small RNA molecule that participates in protein synthesis. Each tRNA molecule has two important areas: a trinucleotide region called the anticodon and a region for attaching a specific amino acid. During translation, each time an amino acid is added to the growing chain, a tRNA molecule forms base pairs with its complementary sequence on the messenger RNA (mRNA) molecule, ensuring that the appropriate amino acid is inserted into the protein.[8]

2) Vesicles, Target Acquisition — The Secret Weapon

A vesicle is a self-contained structure consisting of fluid or gas surrounded and enclosed by an outer membrane called the lipid bilayer. This is made up of hydrophilic heads but hydrophobic tails that cluster together. The heads are more like propellers or swimmers given their natural affinity for water, and the tails maybe more like paddles or rudders given the lack of affinity. These microscopic vesicles have the appearance of tiny globules, blood plasma like, that store and transport material that an organism needs to survive and recycle waste materials. They can also absorb

---

[8] Ibid.

and destroy toxic substances and pathogens to prevent cell damage and infection.

Just like humans were created uniquely, vesicles within us have unique functions and abilities. For example, they can fuse with the membranes of other cells to carry out a specific role, such as breaking down another cell. Vesicles also help store and transport materials such as proteins, enzymes, hormones, and neurotransmitters. They are a small but essential part of biological systems and processes such as: digestion and metabolism, the nervous system, and kidney and liver function.

In molecular biology, we discover that God designed the factories and transport vehicles for production and logistics so that transport vesicles in the cell transports biologically produced materials from one part of a cell to another and extracellular regions. Consider microscopic vesicles, vital to the mission of life itself in protein trafficking, which is the transport and movement of proteins throughout the cell or from the cell to the extracellular environment. Manufactured proteins are packaged and loaded into transport vesicles and moved from the production facility, rough endoplasmic reticulum, to the Distribution Center (DC), biologically known as the Golgi apparatus where additional sorting and refining takes place before final packaging is done specifically depending upon their final destination within the manufacturing and distribution/logistics or delivery process. In molecular biology terms, delivery is translocation.

The process involves the signal recognition particle pathway of protein translocation into the endoplasmic reticulum (ER). The signal recognition particle (SRP) binds to its receptor (SR) in the ER membrane as well as to the docked ribosome. The translocon contains proteins to be trafficked and the translocation requires GTP hydrolysis (+GTP - a chemical decomposition process adding the elements of H_2O), enabling the carrier to propel itself to its destination.

We have manufacturing and logistics companies which you work at, have worked at or have supported in some way around the world for countless products, and it's genius that started the whole process right inside our own bodies. That could only be done with a wisely laid out plan and awesome power to bring it to fruition. Now, we humans copy the Master's ingenuity, and as they say, "Flattery gets you everywhere." The comparison is mind blowing, and the focus of the plan is none other than the future. God, the creator, isn't done yet. People die everyday, every hour, so does 50 to 70 billion cells per person. How do the microorganisms keep up with reproduction at that rate requiring breakneck speeds refreshing our bodies? They do it tirelessly as God commanded. There is a microscopic helicase that spins at the speed of a turbine jet engine unraveling DNA all day, all night. Imagine that! Why? Because God said so.

3) Nanoparticles

Nanoparticles, introduced by biotech companies decades ago, are now center stage in playing the field with molecular biological agents of life itself to solve problems introduced naturally that we cannot combat well. The problem is not necessarily only the drug or medicine unavailability, but logistics of safely delivering the medicine to the exact cell region in the body to fight a naturally caused virus at its highest potency, given toxic combat zones that can breakdown the vaccine and medicine sent in to war. These soldiers need protection to get to the target safely, not so different than soldiers on the battlefields of the middle-east and other militant regions of the world.

Look at it like this. When President Obama authorized the Navy Seals to go into the small town of Abbottobad, Pakistan to take out Osama Bin Laden, the intel on the ground had taken years to develop. The Navy seals transported in Blackhawk helicopters were vulnerable and could have been intercepted and met with ballistics that could have blown them out of the sky as they approached Bin Laden's compound. That would have seriously degraded the mission and left the Seals in enemy territory, dead or alive just like the microorganisms and acid conditions of the molecular war zone. In fact, even though the team followed a well practiced plan of target acquisition, strike, and extraction at ground zero, one of the helicopters experienced mechanical failure, clipping a tall wall surrounding the compound, crashed and was disabled. Solving the problem of delivery to molecular structures in our body is comparable but even more lethal.

So Biotechs have studied and tested nanotechnology in labs developing test vaccines and attack plans based on nature's own packaging and delivery technology beginning with lipid nanoparticles. Lipid biomolecules are one of the four "molecules of life." Lipid nanoparticles are the fatty molecular envelopes (the genetic ferry boat like transport vesicles) that assist strands of mRNA (messenger RNA) to evade the body's biological security defense system advancing to the target cell without fear of degradation. With the nature of mRNA's role of manufacturing DNA code into proteins for delivery, cellular and extracellular, these nanoparticles are the key to the success of specific cellular home address delivery of the most advanced and phenomenal technologies incorporated in vaccines and drugs today and for the foreseeable future.

Nanoparticles are now in the test labs using nanotechnology to ferry the genome-editing CRISPR-Cas9 to target organs themselves. This would be a breakthrough as it would expand the use to solve other delivery challenges, ferrying into hostile territory.

This ferry is a derivative of our Creator's molecular biological technology from creation, transport vesicles — can we say that history, the past, is crucial to the outcome of a plan for the future? It's a statement, not a question --- immensely rhetorical.

4) Advances in Nano-Medicine

The FDA's approval of the first RNAi-based drug was "proof these nanoparticles were not just tools we use in the lab to manipulate genes," Anderson said in a STAT Report on nanomedicine, "but proof they can be translated into approved medicines."

A nanocarrier system made up of lipid or polymeric nanoparticles can bring mRNA into cells to instruct them to make antigens and stimulate the immune system to make antibodies against SARS-CoV-2. These lipids and polymers are designed to escape enzymes that might rapidly degrade the mRNA, keeping them most effective. And that has taken decades to develop with the future in mind.

Nanomaterials could also play a key role in getting vaccines to people in resource-poor or densely populated countries. Vaccines could one day be administered through microneedle patches, single-dose slow-release implants, film-based nanomaterials, or plant viral nanoparticles for antigen delivery, which do not require cold chains. That's the hopes of the "desirable future quadrant."

Nanomedicine has a bright future in molecular stimulation of protein production in that new possibilities are knocking at the door of breakthrough in that it is a critical aide to rendering protective transport of mRNA vaccines, but it is also key in reformulating existing drugs and formulating new ones to treat Covid-19 patients. "In my mind, one of the heroes in this story is the RNA nanoparticle," said Daniel Anderson, professor of chemical engineering at the Massachusetts Institute of Technology, because "siRNA led to mRNA vaccines."[9]

---

[9] COONEY, ELIZABETH, How nanotechnology helps mRNA Covid-19 vaccines work, DECEMBER 1, 2020 Reprints, BIOTECH, STAT Reports: Nanotechnology in Medicine,https://www.statnews.com/2020/12/01/how-nanotechnology-helps-mrna-covid19-vaccineswork/

Before Covid-19 spread around the globe, mRNA vaccines were in the early stages of development in biotech companies, and nanoscience and nanotechnology was central to their efforts.

"After all, viruses are naturally occurring nanoparticles, and indeed, the nanotechnology community has long been trying to capitalize on the properties of viruses and mimic their behavior, for example, for the design of virus-like nanoparticles for targeted drug delivery and gene editing," (an editorial in Nature Nanotechnology) [10]

The potential here is revolutionary in that securely packaged mRNA into vaccines which direct encoding of DNA to manufacture the "spike" protein lurking on the surface of the novel coronavirus initiates the natural biomolecular production of that key protein, spurring an immune system reaction certain to train cells to effectively fight the virus which would be a big win in the prevention of Covid-19. With the release of the vaccine, Moderna and Pfizer-BioNTech COVID 19, in record time, we seem to be very very close and on the road to perfecting this attack strategy even though initial deployment of the vaccine is less than stellar and as more vaccines are being introduced. In contrast to mimicking disease components to trick the immune system into building defenses against future infections with the real thing, mRNA vaccines jump-start cellular protein-making machinery to fight the invader by creating a piece of the spike protein found on the surface of the coronavirus. And when I say machinery, I mean just that because our bodies have gazillions of biomolecular factories designed by God to keep us alive and functioning properly.

In it's progression of a plan that started decades ago based on technology introduced by the creator thousands of years ago, it clearly follows the pattern of focus: past, present, unknown and future desires.

---

[10] Ibid

Vaccines derived from mRNA is not an unknown as it has been tested for decades with the flu, Zika, rabies, and cytomegalovirus (CMV).[11]

It's a different technique from the one used by traditional vaccines and has gained serious ground and popularity given the ability to test in laboratories with the convenience of materiel availability.

As I write this book, mRNA vaccines are upfront, center stage, on a frontier which confronts nature in nanomedicine in the fight against Covid-19, but that's not my focus, nor yours. Our Focus is to understand what our focus should be to reach our Highest Good. This complex challenge just happens to be a magnificent champion of age old technology from the annals of creation history to the here and now with greater plans and hopes of success in medicine for the far future, regardless and because of the not so unknown. Having said that, I'd like to cement history with this next statement. "The biggest vaccination campaign in history is underway. More than 213 million doses have been administered across 95 countries, according to data collected by Bloomberg as of February 24, 2021 [more than double that — 457 MM in 134 countries as of March 22nd]. The latest rate was roughly 6.11 million doses a day [almost double that — 11.3 MM as of March 22nd]. In America alone, at this time more than 65 million doses have been administered and an average of 1.28 million doses over the past week was administered per day [practically doubling that — 127 MM doses and an avg of 2.49MM over the past week as of March 22nd]."[12] And that, as expected to increase tremendously in the 1st and 2nd quarter of 2021, is performing as projected by the new presidential administration, oldest president in history, Joe Biden and first female, first Black and American Indian Vice-president in history, Kamala Harris. Obviously, these stats will increase even though vaccination delivery is not

---

[11] YOUR HEALTH, Understanding mRNA COVID-19 Vaccines, Updated Dec. 18, 2020, https://www.cdc.gov/coronavirus/2019-ncov/vaccines/different-vaccines/mrna.html
[12] Bloomberg vaccine tracker. https://www.bloomberg.com/

meeting expectation or demand as more companies are awaiting FDA approval, so accuracy as of the day or year you read this is not the point.

So what is the point, the moral of this story? Plan and Focus on the Future with the aid of yesterday while acting today. It's that important, yet so simple.

The brain is so complex that, even today, we have no clue as to where the mind resides as it is not physically present within the brain as we know it. Artificial Intelligence and Nanotechnology are so far advanced because the architectures look to the future through binoculars of the beginning of time, and that allows focused concentration on solving medical problems of the here and now. Call it "the ecosystem of time" if you will, all are connected.

So, again, Focus for the individual is partitioned into 4 quadrants, ***the past, the present, the desirable future, and the unknown***, and they are all key to the greatest probability of attaining the Highest Good of the Individual and a well managed future outcome.

The ending is all that we have in common with every outcome. Plan all the particulars incorporating your end goal, effecting and protecting your dream or a variant thereof, taking into account all the known possible deterrents, twists of fate and fortune, hurdles and detours that might reroute your plan as you know it. By tactical and strategic planning all the way to your desirable future, you will be better prepared to execute plan A, B or C near term and long term. And when you have reached your goal, you will be wise to settle down, put the brakes on, and build a "virtual fortress" around your prize, not yourself; but remain guarded! If you think far ahead, you will be many steps ahead of your contemporaries, potential problems, and foes, organic or not.

"There are very few men—and they are the exceptions—who are able to think and feel beyond the present moment."[13] Carl von Clausewitz, 1780-1831

Don't worry so much about overplanning and rigidity because that approach is far more productive than lack of planning and constant impromptu, reactionary behavior in the face of danger. The only caution concerning overplanning is that sometimes we are stricken with analysis paralysis and never construct a viable plan, time eaten away by termites of indecisiveness in that we spin our wheels overthinking a situation, never putting our good foot forward to effect a plan at all.

"Perfect is the enemy of good."[14] So at some point, we must make a good decision based on current knowledge, target immediate reasonable gains with tactical actions relying on current and anticipated resources, and allow time to cure the strategic plan. Trade-in the tendency to improvise circumstantially for tactical and strategic planning all the way to your end-goal, then when you reach your end-goal, be smart; pause and implement your end-game.

"There is no real purpose in contemplating a reversal to this Law, then, for no good can come from refusing to think far into the future and planning to the end. If you are clear- and far thinking enough, you will understand that the future is uncertain, and that you must be open to adaptation. Only having a clear objective and a far-fetching plan allows you that freedom."[15] Robert Greene

Timidity has no place in your approach and execution of a well designed strategy. Be bold in your approach. Boldness is highly preferred in

---

[13] Greene, Robert, 48 Laws of Power, Plan All the Way to the End, Carl von Clausewitz, 1780-1831, pg 237

[14] Trionfo, Victor (Alias), Editor in Chief, 2001

[15] Greene, Robert, 48 Laws of Power, Plan All the Way to the End, pg 244

relation to timidity because it is respected by those that will court you on your ascension to success and, therefore, immensely effective in achieving unprecedented results. Build your plan with strict timelines and milestones. While rigidity may seem inflexible, it is actually preferred to improvisation at every turn. The combination of boldness and rigidity will net you greater success in the shortest timespan. Boldness looks and smells of confidence and success.

Heightened awareness renders deeper levels of confidence that influence the ability to stand in the truth of who one believes themselves to be, irrespective of what others might think. And actually a bold, more confident you elicits greater respect opening doors you may not have even anticipated. The authentic self then becomes no longer willing to compromise what is true in its own sphere to satisfy the opinions of others. Living in that space releases a person from the need of validation or permission from anyone other than self, and, yet, it gains respect of those championing your plan.

The art of being bold and unapologetic in one's total truth liberates him from the prison of other people's denigrating opinions and their own fears. It may work to your detriment to pretend to be something other than what you are, merely for the sake of gaining acceptance of others. When a person is true to themselves, they allow their individuality to permeate their surroundings and govern their thoughts and behavior. Being true to self takes courage and requires introspection, sincerity, an open-mind, and fairness. The truest nature of a person's spirit is peace. The enemy will try at every turn to steal, kill, and destroy that peace. That is why it is imperative that one be willing to adapt, making necessary adjustments to secure it at all costs.

Peace of mind, while not absent conflict, harnesses the power to cope with chaos while remaining steadfast in those things that are favorable. Accepting the truth of the moment and denying the voice of the ego is the best route to real peace, living in the true essence of the soul. Ego is self-serving, and it's only concern is what and how something is going to gratify itself. The soul's genuine desire is to live and be harmonious in all things. It does not find gratification in discord. Genuine change begins and ends with self. Even if things do not change on the outside, peace comes from making things change from within.

The more an individual becomes in-tune with that which resonates with them on a spirit level, the more that person will disconnect from causation of chaos and unrest. In a spirit of harmony, the disconnect does not have to be hostile. It encompasses anything done in grace upon the wings of God, so making the choice to jettison or disengage will net you significant gain. It is quite possible to put distance between oneself and those things or persons that subject them to feelings of discontentment by disallowing any hostility to occur during the separation, which is a sign of true growth.

iv. Emotional intelligence Ei or EQ

Emotional intelligence or EI is the ability to understand and manage your own emotions and those of the people around you. A high degree of emotional intelligence indicates that one has perfect knowledge of what they're feeling, the ability to access one's own emotions while determining their meaning, and the ability to pre-diagnose how these emotions can affect those in the effecting vicinity and at the receiving end of the emotions.

Controlling anger is not always the easiest thing to do. Anger is an emotion that needs immediate attention. It is not patient. It is untamed and rages as it shouts truth about its pain. Mastering the ability to control anger takes tremendous patience and willpower. It is acceptable to feel and express anger because it is a valid emotion, but we must learn to express it in a way received constructively by others.

"Anybody can become angry–that is easy, but to be angry with the right person and to the right degree and at the right time and for the right purpose, and in the right way - that is not within everybody's power and is not easy." **Aristotle**

Aristotle was essentially making the case for emotional intelligence and its prominence in everything we do. The way I view it is that Emotional IQ requires an emotional poker face;

"You gotta know when to hold'em, know when to explode'em."

It's an art. Without mastering the art of emotion management, one cannot master the art of life of least resistance, greatest positive human effect, and greatest success at whatever is beside and ahead of you. Nor can one master best outcome of one's actions of situational dependency. Lastly, success in anything from making the best decision including business, leadership, finances, and day to day challenges to deciding what's best in your relations with friends and romances, depend on mastering the art of Emotional IQ. So what is it in the most succinct manner I can propose?

Emotional IQ is the litmus test of perfect awareness of one's own emotions and that of those in his purview and is the preeminent determinant for the success of the individual in business and relationships.

Succinct enough? Listen, Aristotle's statement is dead presidents! Translation: dead on the money, no pun intended — well, maybe a little bit. It's not DOA and certainly not only for negative emotions, but for any emotion, period. We must manage emotions in the right way, at the right time, and for the right purpose. Our outward response to inner emotions is an act expressing the way in which securing the needs of the individual are attempted, and they provide us with perceived necessary information craved or desired. Emotions communicate, connecting one to true self and are not necessarily effectively expressed following best practice.

Unconditional acceptance of oneself is also about understanding that all emotions, whatever they may be, are valid. Just as we measure how smart we are with Intelligence Quotient (IQ) tests, MCAT, the Bar Exam, SAT and PSAT tests etc., there are tests to determine your intelligence of your emotions, Emotional intelligence (Ei). One such test is the Mayer-Salovey-Caruso Emotional Intelligence Test in which you receive a score, not unlike an IQ test (which has its own set of controversies). According to University of New Hampshire professor of psychology, John D. Mayer, Ei is one's ability to accurately perceive their own and others' emotions, to understand the signals that emotions send about relationships, and to manage your own and others' emotions.

Believe it or not, there are arguments which, based on a few studies, indicate that predictably, your Ei is a better indicator of potential success than your IQ. That makes good sense, actually. Now whether that stands when the comparison is fully vetted with data for years or decades, remains to be seen, but a high IQ does not one make hugely successful nor exempt from failure in life. In the same sense, having an Emotional IQ that's off the grid means that you can apply it in everything around you significantly, and that leads to tremendous success. Now an author, Daniel Goleman, a Psychologist and Science Journalist with Reporter for The New York Times on his CV, the champion of emotional intelligence concluded the same.

So naturally, we're curious about the correlation. Well, you've heard the colloquial phrase, "I laugh in the face of danger." However simple that seems, it's actually rather complex and not necessarily innate. To be able to control your emotions under fire is an incredible feat. So if it isn't innate, where does it come from? It can be innate, but if it isn't, it can be learned.

For leaders, having emotional intelligence is vitally essential for success. I've always been told that the CEO of many companies is the C+ student, and I never connected Ei to their success. I just thought that they may have been the most popular in their class and happened to be more charismatic, surrounding themselves with bright talent. Ok, I wasn't far off, but Emotional Intel never once popped into my head. You do not have to be the Einstein, Nikola Tesla, or Elon Musk of the Organization to reach tremendous success. In fact, Einstein is said to have wasted the last 30 or so years of his life as he became detached from the mainstream Physics community in quixotic aspirations of demystifying a new theory or discipline known to us as quantum mechanics. His struggle ended in disappointment in attempting the creation of his Unified Field Theory of describing all the forces of nature, although he did leave perplexing questions for science that proliferates and vibrates throughout the discipline of physics even today.

But the strange thing to the likes of the accomplished Danish Physicist, Niels Bohr, is that Einstein was really the progenitor of quantum mechanics as he was awarded the Nobel Prize of Physics for his incredible work in proving the existence of energy particles in light which ignited the pathway to the discovery of quantum mechanics in physics where newly discovered microscopic particles that are also waves moving at the speed of light exist in no specific place until measured. Sounds crazy, right? "My point exactly," Einstein would probably say, "Does a tree make a sound when it falls in the Appalachian Mountains if no one is there to hear it, nor device to record the sound?" My point is that this is the approach which Einstein took, railing against the grain of what today is scientifically supported, and he did so, trying from 1927 until his death in 1955, to debunk a theory which he spawned. He attempted this while latching onto the restraints defined in the Uncertainty Principle, attempting things like disproving the existence of black holes altogether through combining gravity, a force we still do not understand fully today, with the force of electromagnetism due to his success with the theory of relativity. But he found that as gravitational forces became much stronger, even light couldn't escape black holes which was a stab in the heart of his years of work to go against quantum mechanics. So, I believe that as stated earlier, Einstein engaged and was married to a quixotic approach of low emotional IQ which overrode his IQ as a mythic god in the world of physics. In 1982 Niels Bohr's theory would prevail, as he was vindicated by research accomplished by a French physicist disproving the theories of Einstein that quantum mechanics was immanently flawed.[16]

Nikola Tesla, whom Tesla, Inc. (formerly Tesla Motors) is named after, was way ahead of his time as an inventor and engineer who sold his patents of the most critical electric concepts in history to George Westinghouse. The Serbian American inventor discovered and patented the rotating magnetic field central to the basis of most alternating-current (AC) machinery, a system of AC dynamos, transformers, and motors. In 1891, he invented the Tesla coil, widely used in radio technology, and even invented the first wireless lighting system. Yet sadly, he struggled and died a very poor man. The founders of Tesla Motors, CEO Martin Eberhard and CFO Marc Tarpenning, on the other hand, realised that the company needed a genius Product Architect to catapult them to electrifying success and hired Elon Musk, founder and former Paypal CEO, as their technical brainiac, and the rest is history — for that matter, future simultaneously! Despite the fact that Eberhard and Tarpenning both left Tesla in 2008, the point is that a High IQ does not necessarily make one successful — accomplished maybe, but not for certain successful. Spin that another direction on the wheel of life, and we can say boldly that relationship success is predicated on a high score in Ei. After all, who is more likely to succeed, one who wildly expresses emotions through acts of fits and rage or one who processes the emotions he or she is feeling and acts proactively and informatively, unlike one who reacts without thought or care of the effect on those targeted because of the emotion? The pro usually wins.

---

[16] https://www.discovermagazine.com/the-sciences/einsteins-grand-quest-for-a-unified-theory

Daniel Goleman as an Ei champion helped to popularize emotional intelligence, applying five key elements to it:

Self-awareness

Self-regulation

Motivation (for relationships, think Motive) Empathy

Social skills

Emotional Intelligence in Relationships

1. Self-awareness

If you're self-aware, you always know how you feel, and you know how your emotions and your actions can affect the people around you. Being self-aware when you're in a relationship positions you to present yourself in the most positive light, having a clear picture of your strengths and weaknesses, and it means behaving with kindness and humility.

2. Self-regulation

Partners who effectively regulate themselves rarely attack others verbally or attempt to invalidate each other's feelings. Nor are they quick tempered, making rash decisions from spoiled emotions, pass judgment, or compromise either their or their partner's values by crossing border lines without a passport. Self-regulation is all about respect and staying in control.

Personal accountability, key to forgiveness and healing for both offender and the victim, is a strong characteristic of self regulation. Know your values and stick to them, including your code of ethics and boundaries. Hold yourself accountable without question, face the consequences, and do it quickly. It will make a tremendous difference in how your partner, friends, and acquaintances see you, respond to you, and reciprocate.

3. Motive

You must know and be deeply immersed in the attraction that magnetized you to the relationship. You should be keen on the motive in your estimation and a pattern that can be seen in your partner or friends to have a relationship with you. When your relationship sours from mistakes made on either part, and you trod to a therapist or counselor, one of the first questions asked will be, Are you willing to continue this relationship? A close second will be, "What attracted you in the first place, and can you state and write down 5 positive things that your partner does that you admire? These are typical questions asked if the relationship is on the brinks but not shattered, therefore salvageable. That should be in the forefront of all action and problem solving.

Re-examine why you engaged in the relationship. If you're unhappy in your relationship and feel threatened in any way, then you should probably head toward the exit corridor on your escape plan.

If all motives are sincere, then you should realise that nothing is perfect, no one is perfect, and that includes you. Lean towards working it out, and where there is difficulty figuring out root cause, use a technique that Six Sigma uses, the Five Whys technique which is awesomely effective. It's like peeling back the layers of the onion with authority of deeper introspection to find the "rot" cause. Yes, r-o-t causation.

Always know where you stand in the relationship, be optimistic, find something good even if it's small or subtle with which you can repair. But know the motive, and don't be fooled or forced. If you find that love and respect lives within and just need dusting off, it's well worth the effort.

4. Empathy

Make empathy central to your relationship because it is critical to managing success and your own emotions. Being empathic is having the capacity and, therefore, ability to put oneself in someone else's situation, to feel what your partner feels, causing you to sympathize with them and offer comfort or relief in an appropriate fashion where necessary. Expressed empathetic feelings go a long way in developing a relationship of honesty, trust and solidarity. It promotes grace, mercy, fairness and acceptance. It helps you to challenge those being accusatory and acting callously and unfairly towards the subject of empathy. One trait that you must possess and display is being a good listener audibly and emotionally.

If you want to earn the respect and loyalty of your mate or friends, then show them, really show them, when it's tough that you care by being empathic. Meditate and put yourself in someone else's position in an attempt to try and see their point of view. After all, you benefit by taking the time to look at situations from other people's perspectives. Be perceptive, pay your diligent dues by paying attention to their body language, but be mindful of yours as well so that there is no misperception of your genuine interest, concern, or care when listening. Learning to read body language and give off the right signals can be a real asset in fostering great relations, because you'll be better able to determine how someone truly feels and ensure that they receive your mannerisms in the fashion you intend.

5. Social Skills

Partners and friends with very good social skills tend to be very efficient communicators. A great communicator must be a great listener and a great judge of character. Being perceptive is everything, and knowing your audience and interfacing accordingly ensures unbroken connections. Bad news is just as essential to one with great social skills as the good news. If I know the bad news, I can plan around it, but if it comes late or not at all, it could cause irreparable disaster. Conflict resolution will be a strong suit for the nimbly skilled, socially.

These five elements sum up why emotional intelligence is so important and effective if mastered. Empathy is big in relationships as well as motive. Catering to others' needs is only possible if you know what your capacity is to perform the catering service. So the emotions and desires as well as boundaries are essential for great communications and relations for all involved. That way, rarely does one get their feelings stepped on, nor does anyone get taken advantage of intentionally. Getting in touch with your emotions and those of people around you can change your life significantly with amazing gain of prosperity.

The mirror reflected me as never having been any good at managing my emotions. I would, and still do sometimes, go from zero to a 1000 in a matter of minutes, and I wasn't even equipped with a supersonic jet engine. Things would always get to me. It's easy to paint me in this light because I am a very passionate person, and I feel my emotions strongly, but there is no excuse for losing control and flying off the handle. Learning how to control my emotions is still a struggle, but, daily, I attempt to get better at managing them and not allowing them to manage me.

Growth in life is an ongoing process, and I am realizing better ways to manage and express my emotions. It is true, I can be raw in my expression as I have many times been told. I'll be the first to admit I was and still can be quick-tempered, but there must be better ways for me to express my feelings without putting other people on guard. That was never my strong suit. If it came up, it was coming out, no holds barred. Frequently, my ego would not allow me to hear the truth of those statements of how my delivery was insensitive. So, my delivery is sometimes my focus, and, other times, I miss the mark and just speak my uncensored piece of mind. Sometimes, you just have to say it how you feel it, and I am doing my best to know that is not always the best practice.

I should use my emotions as indicators of what is happening inside my mind and heart, and I don't announce every one of them. We were beings who had feelings before we were beings who became thinkers. Having the ability to feel makes a person human. Emotions connect a person to their humanity. There are some who like to use the colloquialism, "get out your feelings." That statement alone forces people to diminish their humanness and take on a state of robotic living. It is essential that one allows themselves to experience their feelings. In my estimation, denying one's feelings is like denying one's humanness. The key is to not remain stagnant in those emotions that prevent a person's ability to operate from a place of grace while preserving the nature of one's existence as an imperfect creature. Listening to and understanding one's emotions is the basis of knowing one's self. People are allowing society to condition themselves to believe that it is wrong to experience and express feelings.

The whole concept about "being in your feelings" is not the best idea and opens the door for denial of self. There is another expression that the millennia have caused to spread like wildfire, "feel some type of way." This idiom prohibits the individual from giving meaning to their emotions, crippling them in having the ability to identify what it is that they are feeling, further causing them to lose an opportunity to learn and understand self on a deeper level. The experience of emotion keeps one in-tune with the truth of who they are and how they show up in life. It should always be a rule of thumb to be open and honest about what is being felt, at least with self if no one else. Only then can one truly manage their emotions which, by the way, gives them the license to recognize and manage the emotions of others surrounding them. That is quintessential emotional intelligence.

Being honest with oneself begins and continues with becoming totally aware of emotions and accepting of self. As intelligence of one's and others' emotions increases, serenity and peace with others and unconditional love fill the heart, then holistic acceptance of who you are and must be to manage interactions with others becomes the new norm. For most of my life, I put more trust in what people thought than what I believed and frankly what my emotions revealed. I had to be sure that people only saw me in the best light. For me, that meant diminishing my own emotions defining what mattered to me giving way only to that which others' emotions dictated, cancelling my emotions from the equation. It didn't matter what I wanted to them, and I fell hook, line and sinker. To a degree, my feelings didn't matter if it meant I could avoid conflict of any kind. So, I wore a mask to hide those parts of me that I felt they thought were less appealing and would ridicule. I masked emotions, suppressing any frequency that I felt would not vibe with them to my own detriment. I would hide behind the masqueraded version of myself to appease the hunger palate of the emotions for the thrill of the taste of who they expected me to be.

There were parts of me I kept hidden for so long, wonderful parts, not so wonderful parts, stoic parts, just OK parts, but my — my parts — authentically me parts. I relished in this ritual sufficiently enough to erase the true essence of who I was. Social conditioning has a way of causing a person to lose sight of themselves. The fear of being mocked and feeling judged were the primary reasons I frequented masquerading behavior. Hiding my vulnerabilities and lashing out in anger to protect those parts of me that were in jeopardy of being hurt became "Operation Practice Normale'." I silenced the screams of my thirsting emotions, despite their parched lips and hunger pains because I didn't want anyone to think of me as needy and insecure. Truth be told, Insecure was easily my middle name. I was insecure because I thought something was wrong with me. I wanted to parade a certain image of impermeability, but the day came when I didn't want to keep displaying a façade, and it occurred to me that I shouldn't have shortchanged me to satisfy the misapplied standards of others. Realizing that my weaknesses do not define me, nor my insecurities make me less deserving of love and respect, liberated me and gave me the strength to honor my emotions as well as stand in my truth no matter what others thought.

Wearing that covering and concealing the truth of who I was and dampening my true emotional character, in essence, discarding how I felt, was quite deceitful to self. Restricting yourself from your own truth is ineffective and counterproductive. I learned to live and follow what I felt was best for me, even if it were a mistake. It would be my mistake and my choice, and I needed to learn to manage my decisions with guidance from God alone. I began paying more attention to and understanding myself so much so, it became acceptable to set my own standard and be loyal to me and my best interest. For the longest time, I hesitated out of fear, opening myself and my heart to others because I didn't want to face the fear of being left alone. At one point or another, I have felt abandoned by quite a few people, and I wore the badge of fear that anybody I loved would either not love me back or leave me. That was a dangerous emotion, and I didn't have the emotional IQ to realise it.

So, I did what I could to protect myself from feeling the pain of being abandoned and alone. Ironically, the more I did to hold on to people, the more it seemed I would lose them. The reality of living with that shield of protection around my heart was that I was not giving love the opportunity to flow out or in. This was the stepchild of emotional blocking. That lifestyle recognizably became problematic as I always ended up picking up the shattered pieces of an already bruised heart alone.

Emotional blocking is the activity one uses to protect themselves from the weight of what they might feel in stressful situations. I cover emotional blocking in greater detail later, but for now, suffice it to say it serves as a defense mechanism. This mechanism acts as a buffer to block all or part of an emotion so that one can regain some semblance of normalcy. The individual uses emotional blocking to give them a chance to process their emotions a little bit at a time.

Even though I had to nurse a wounded heart, I was aware enough to realise and mature enough to admit that I was the common denominator in all my failed relationships. That realisation meant it was time to figure out just what it was about my character that was causing me to fail in relationships. Since I was the common denominator, it was time to look at that faded reflection in the mirror and make sense of how I was showing up in the world and in my relationships. So, I did what most are not willing to do, and that is to look in the mirror and try to understand the faded and emotionally disconnected reflection that stared back at me. Focusing my attention on areas of my life that were stagnant and figuring out the things or thoughts that were hindering me from blossoming into the full essence of who God created me to be became my priority. And with this inclination of renewed focus, my emotional intelligence skyrocketed. The revelation I had was that not only was I disconnected from others, I disconnected from myself inciting deprivation of emotions.

When healing becomes a top priority, finding the courage to free oneself of their own dysfunctional tendencies can be frightening at first but very much liberating. The journey of self-discovery is more so about acknowledging and understanding all dimensions of one's own personality. We are multidimensional beings, and we achieve true wholeness when we can honor and accept every part of ourselves beyond the shadow of a doubt. The key to living in alignment is the total acceptance of self, mind, body, and spirit which is in square when the plumb line of the head and the heart is perfectly straight. Misalignment creeps in through the crawl space of inner conflict when the head and heart are not in agreement and erraticism prevails.

Clarity is one of the perquisites of living in alignment. Being in touch with one's own emotions and being keen on how their reactions to those emotions impact others opens up brave and bold activity within the brain attracting amazing success, love, and acceptance to oneself.

Understanding who one believes themselves to be is phenomenally profitable, and the peace garnered from living in that belief is immeasurable.

All too often people allow themselves to attach to someone else's emotions and the fantasy of who that person thinks they should be, and it only ends in suppression, suffocation, and depression for the individual. Accepting all things about self takes the power away from those who harbor malicious intent. When we deny or refrain from fully accepting certain parts of our own personality, we fall out of balance and lose control. A person cannot operate in the true authenticity of who they believe themselves to be when they deny certain parts of themselves to appease others.

v. Authentically Me -- The Creator's Creature

I wanted to connect directly to my Creator, my source, God. Doing so meant I had to understand that I am not separate from my source. God lives within me, and I am connected to the infinite just as the infinite is connected to me. I redefine myself by first giving myself permission to feel the vibrations of my own inner spirit. I had to learn how to listen to my own soul. I was no longer afraid to live in the authenticity of who I was and desired to be. I no longer gave other people authority over my emotions and to determine what was right for me. It wasn't a change that took place over night, as the self is continually growing. Growth is constant and lifelong (-asmos is the suffix for continual in Greek as we will see later), so changes or modifications to my behavior and principles will change as I continue to evolve into greater versions of myself. I was open and honest first with myself and after that became openly honest with others. That was the hardest decision to stand on, the one decision that truly does define me, to be and present to the world, me authentically. I gained the power to stand true to my genuine feelings regardless of what anyone else thought. I had been so used to masquerading my feelings to agree with the crowd that I would deny what was true for me just to fit in. But I could no longer disguise, suppress, restrict, color, dress down, or deny my authentic emotions. I just couldn't do it anymore, because It was gaining me nothing, in fact, my P&L statement reflected a horrifying net loss due to minuscule profit and overwhelming loss. I found the courage and the strength to stand strong in my convictions, even if it meant I had to stand alone. It took bravery for me to do that, and I experienced some lonely and restless days and nights, but I knew there had to be an upside to all this, a greater prophetic meaning for all I had endured. I discontinued talking about the things I felt, because I had grown tired of being told I was wrong before I could ever finish what I was trying to say.

Everybody was so quick to tell me how wrong I was! I was judging myself enough from the confusion in my own head, so judgment from others simply exacerbated the madness of it all. It was in those moments that I realised I needed friends, not judges. I made a promise to myself not to let people leave my presence or conversations with me feeling worse than when they approached me. I realise that often I just wanted to be heard, so it became my mission to hear others out fully. I wanted to set the example by being what I needed reciprocated. The more I changed my behavior to become what I needed, the clearer I saw myself. That mirror, of course, revealed things that I didn't initially want to accept, but if I was going to get to the other side of that mountain, I had to make some adjustments to the hiking gear to reach my extraordinary life. I believe the Creator did not his creature create for mediocrity; maybe that's why some things I have had to endure have not been common situations. Common problems come to all, but only extraordinarily complex problems seem to be reserved for extraordinary creations.

Problem is, people are too afraid to just be...authentically be — too busy worrying about what someone is going to say or think. Whatever the experience, a person should not feel they have to deny true self to protect the image they personify. Denying one's true self only proves the inability to live according to the whole truth of his or her soul. If a person is going to live in the whole truth of who they are, they should not deny parts of themselves out of fear of judgment. It is quite possible that different people can share the same experience and have completely different perspectives according to the collective experiences of the individual. That doesn't mean that there is anything wrong with their elected decision, it just means that different people have variable thought processes, and they should not feel like they must deny their decisions simply because others may not approve or see it through their lenses.

I gave of my time and services effortlessly to anyone in need. I made myself available upon request without hesitation. I did what I perceived was needed instead of giving of my true heart. That part of me, I would protect at all cost because I didn't want to bear the pain of "in the moment" rejection or worse, abandonment. It just became easier and safer to mask the fruit of my heart. I avoided opening my heart and my true self to people out of fear, so it became normal to operate from my head and not my heart. The funny thing is, I told myself that I was operating from my heart and had the audacity to get angry when that notion was challenged. The more I tried to protect my already wounded heart, the more it suffered bruises. I realise the things I focused on only attracted more of the same. I was so afraid of losing people, it seems I only attracted people who would abandon me.

I equated love to material things. When the mirror revealed to me that that is what I was doing, I sought to determine root cause. "Where did that thought stem from?" An inquisition exposing its reason for existence. I knew it was something that I needed to unlearn because love is not about material things. I never really knew how to express my femininity. Unveiling femininity, I thought, meant that I would appear weak or easily taken advantage of because that one time when I opened my whole heart and revealed my vulnerability, love returned to me void. That experience sent me topsy-turvy causing me to irrationally conclude that love sought would never bear the face of love returned because I wasn't good enough.

For years, I carried that in my spirit until it became ingrained in my essence. I walked through life believing I was not good enough. No question, I internalized that disappointment and stopped expressing my vulnerabilities, needs, or desires. I told myself, if I led by example and gave hopefuls what they needed, they would see what I needed and reciprocate. That proved a horrible assumption, an inevitable trap that would attract people who would take me for granted. It should have occurred to me that other people would not automatically know what I needed if I didn't tell them. I just kept hoping love followed an elliptical path, throwing it out like a boomerang, with an assumed auto-return attribute.

I allowed people who had no real investment in what mattered to me to influence my decisions. Change happened when I stopped trying to be what I was not and focused on becoming more of who I am at my core. The actions of others no longer had any influence on who I was, realizing that their disloyalty had no effect on my capacity to be loyal.

Even when I thought I wasn't learning a thing, I was being taught, and, subconsciously, I received instruction that I would need to summon at the right time in the right mind. Life will present endless distractions, but the charge is to be steadfast, immovable, always abounding, checking the repository of experiences that turn out to be invaluable learning events. Standing firm on what we believe in can sometimes be a struggle, especially when you're like me, as I was always one who allowed my emotions to control everything I said and did. It was necessary to learn to control my emotions as they were fickle and had the potential to render life unbalanced. An imbalanced state of being spawns a chaotic lifestyle. Holding a posture of peace is crucial. The idea is to allow the experiences to flow through with a certain level of ease. The greater purpose should always be the focus. The inimical forces of evil will use many tactics to steal the faith that abides within. It's up to the individual to persevere the storms of life acknowledging that however things turn out, the Creator is in control and it is by God's grace that His creatures move and breathe.

In no way do I mean that it is purposeful to dismiss whatever is being felt. It is necessary to feel whatever one feels; it is just disadvantageous to allow those feelings to govern one's life. It is critical to be gentle and patient with self, and, sadly, too often, people have become overly critical of themselves. It is necessary to learn how not to beat up on self when things don't go as planned. I was and still am notorious for this very thing. One must not allow circumstances to prohibit them from growing into the person the Creator created the creature to be.

Too many people have allowed depression to paralyze them, and that immobility has held them hostage. It is counterproductive living life from a depressed point of reference. Looking at life through distressed lenses only breeds more depression within a labyrinth so complex into which you become so deeply entangled and misdirected that it's hard to find a way out. And even if you are just one turn around the wall of freedom on the path of exiting, it will have become so familiar that it becomes even more difficult to escape. It is so much easier to remain within the confines of familiarity, even when that familiar place is dark with an address of 100 Depression Way. Dementedly, it can be of greater comfort to remain in a harmful state than to step outside of that maze and face unknown territory chancing the experience of alternative pathways of travel, even if the escape route leads to freedom on Felicity Avenue. There is always a better way; we must open self to those alternative ways of being. If one is always on the lookout for threats, that person will always draw to them that which they seek.

Moving to 800 Desires of My Heart at the corner of Felicity Avenue is the commitment I'm making.

vi. Learning and Self-Evolution: Adaptation

Adaptation assumes that there is reason or need to discontinue in the same vain, adjusting to the currency of the immediate environment. Trained response or behavior is learning, growing from one frame of reference of understanding to another more acceptable, desirable, and accommodating vantage point. The ability to begin anew is the basis for self-evolution, becoming a more polished you. We discussed AI and the neural synthesis of human intelligence, the end all with learning and evolving: adaptation. There is virtual similarity with AI in our personal lives, if not exact in the sense aforementioned. The basic concepts of learning and evolving are fundamental to adaptability. Combining learning and evolution with Artificial Neural Networks (ANN's) over the past couple of decades with Evolutionary Algorithms (EA's), including using EA's to evolve ANN connection weights, architectures, learning rules, and input features gained immense success in rendering and still points out rich features in significantly more intelligent systems than relying on ANN or EA alone, not to mention the power of architectures. These forms of adaptation will improve quality of life for you as you reach an optimal level of learning and self-evolution. It puts people on notice that you are totally in tune with who you are and that you are where you want to be emotionally in your growth in that any measure inferior to your evolved state is unlikely to meet your standards of engagement. People can only meet you to the degree in which they have met themselves. No one deserves access to another's authentic self if they prove an inability to operate on a level that is acceptable and respectful. When those basic needs are neglected, it is up to the individual to govern themselves accordingly and jettison those individuals who behave unfavorably.

The pattern I was unwilling to acknowledge was that of not enforcing my boundaries. To be totally honest, I had established no boundaries to enforce whatsoever. In AI and Nanotechnology, we set tolerances to effect boundaries, Without boundaries, respect and "expect" is a myth. The lack of boundaries sends the wrong signal to others that it is acceptable to mistreat and disrespect each other, and I could continue with technological analogy. I just hoped that if I did right by people, they would do right by me. But, I learned through trained response, trial and error, that when dealing with others, hope is just not enough. Imagine simply applying hope to Artificial Intelligence and Nanomedicine using no ANN's, no EA's, and no Nanotechnology. It would be a complete failure. It took my exhaustion in repeated failed attempts to see that I was creating the beast that would devour me. It became apparent that nothing was going to change until I trained my thought process to yield plausible results, then adapt, making adjustments, evolving as I made the change to demand the very best of what I knew I needed, could have, and deserved. There is truth in knowing and understanding one's worth and profit in learning and evolving to the Highest Good of self. We can relate to this necessary evolution in our minds especially when we view the take on AI and it's models including applications in today's day, not just the plain vanilla ANN, but other architectures that have evolved like RNN, GAN, CNN and CAPSNet wrapped around ANN. [17]

The notion of me not being good enough equated to me allowing myself to be a doormat to those I wanted to love me back. Love should never feel like manipulation or abuse. It also does not mean that I must walk on eggshells to ensure that I don't say or do anything to cause one to take flight. Love should not be contingent upon my doing, being, and even

---

[17] Neural Network Concepts, The Complete Guide to Artificial Neural Networks: Concepts and Models, https://missinglink.ai/guides/neural-network-concepts/complete-guide-artificial-neural-netw orks/Artificial Neural Networks (ANN)

saying everything other people expect of me and then taken away when I don't measure up to that expectation.

That hope and belief in the potential of others to do the right thing died in my emotional fatigue fathered by repeated experiences of disappointment. It was time for me to demand the best and accept nothing less. I had to reach a certain phase of my life that gave me the courage to

Generative Adversarial Networks (GAN) allow neural networks to generate photos, paintings and other artifacts that closely resemble real ones created by humans.

A Recurrent Neural Network (RNN) helps neural networks deal with input data that is sequential in nature. For example, written text, video, audio, or multiple events that occur one after the other, as in networking or security analytics. An RNN network accepts a series of inputs, remembers the previous inputs, and with each new input, adds a new layer of understanding.

Convolutional Neural Networks (CNN) have proven very effective at tasks involving data that is closely knitted together, primarily in the field of computer vision. A CNN uses a three-dimensional structure, with three sets of neurons analyzing the three layers of a color image—red, green and blue. It analyzes an image one area at a time to identify important features.

Capsule Neural Network (CAPSNet) is a new architecture proposed in 2017 [to more closely mimic biological neural organization], which aims to solve a problem of Convolutional Neural Networks (CNN). CNNs are good at classifying images, but they fail when images are rotated or tilted, or when an image has the features of the desired object, but not in the correct order or position, for example, a face with the nose and mouth switched around. CAPSNet is based on the concept of neural "capsules". It starts with the convolution step just like a regular CNN. But instead of the pooling step, when the network discovers features in the image, it reshapes them into vectors, "squashes" them using a special activation function, and feeds each feature into a capsule stand against childish and unwarranted behavior. I allowed the people I cared about the most to treat me the worst. What I later learned was that I needed to discontinue taking part if I was going to break those patterns. It was time for me to open the space for new relationships that were natural and mutual.

It is necessary to ask for what we need and hold true to our boundaries insistent upon compliance. If the other person makes an honest effort to adjust, then it should be acknowledged that that person cares about and wants to provide what we need. But if that person does not provide what we need, then it can be concluded that that individual does not care about the needs of anyone but themselves. At that point, we must decide regarding the survival or demise of the relationship. Our partners can only do what we allow. Those who do not respect us do not deserve direct access to us. Thus, the beauty of who we are should physically remain a distant star to them. If anyone wreaks havoc and causes discord with our space, their presence is no longer desirable, and jettisoning becomes opportunistically apropos.

While it is very necessary to give others the space to be who they are, it is one's obligation to demand the space needed to be themselves as well. No one should compromise him or herself to benefit the ego of someone else. Everybody deserves that for themselves first. Not one person should mistreat themselves or allow someone else to mistreat them. One cannot expect to be treated well by others if not treated well by themselves. Humans were created of love by Love, so it is necessary to find and take hold of that inner authentic self for the sake of felicity, gratification, and satisfying peace.

For the longest time, I thought humility meant I was supposed to fade into the shadows and let other people have the spotlight, which was fine because I have never been one to crave the spotlight anyway. Fading in the shadows did not mean that I should abandon myself for the benefit of someone else. Nor did standing in my power mean I was greedy for the spotlight. There is a balance between the two, and I could find that balance without dimming my own light. So, in the days before realizing that truth, I hid because I didn't want to be called conceited or arrogant. From that moment on in grade school when some kid said I thought I was cute or something like that, I told myself if I didn't want people to think I was "stuck up," I had to fall back and not stand out. My personality and heart are larger than life, and I shouldn't have to, in this regard, dim my light so that the light in others may shine. We all have equal opportunity and space to let our light so shine when it comes to relationships.

However, in the business world, prudence tells us that it may be felicitous to perform exceedingly well but refract the brilliant light onto a superior strategically for the benefit of one's own progression. That's where keen discernment is evoked and expertly applied for personal gain of loyalty, advancement, and the embellishment of the one who holds the purse strings, allowing her or him the glory. And what is the origin of this, but the Word of God.

In what we know as the Old Testament and the book of Samuel, David was on the run from King Saul when Saul felt threatened by David and sought to kill him even after having married Saul's daughter. Blessedly, Jonathan, Saul's son, saw fit to warn David so that he may flee safely. David then took a team of men with him to the wilderness keeping a low profile. While stealthily roaming the wilderness, he witnessed bandits preying on the livestock of Nabal, a very rich man, and attacked them, thereby protecting the man's livestock. This, he did from his heart and of his own fruition. But it led in David's mind to a lord-vassal agreement between himself and Nabal. In legal terms, it was an imagined quid pro quo agreement. For David's services, he and his men would gain food for life sustainment.

Imagine this as a landlord-tenant agreement in its simplest form. The King was the lord and David the vassal, or the vessel by which the required work of the king was carried out so that gloriously, he remained rich and even grew in wealth from David and his men's protective grunt work, handiwork, albeit David's initiative. This king would shine brilliantly and David and his men would be the low-key or dimmed source of that brilliance. In turn, they would be spared having to risk exposure to King Saul by going to town for food which they could not afford.

But that's not where the rubber met road, and not where rubber meets road today. We shine for the glory of God, not ourselves. We bless Elohim, our creator, in every powerfully successful accomplishment. Glory be to God. We refract the glory away from self and onto God. We have the ultimate Lord-Vassal covenant or contract with the Most High God, King of kings, And in all that we do in his name, we attribute the "Brilliant Shine" to him for his glory, and through this representation and service as an inferior entity, we are blessed having dimmed our light of glory to allow His to shine brilliantly.

And so, the quintessence of humility can be seen in this light, His dimmed light as deity; Jesus walked the face of the earth and exhibited all the attributes of humility: Humble, modesty, down-to-earth, lowliness, submissiveness — and..let's see, Weakness too? — yeah, no, not at all. Rather meekness is what his presence commanded. His example should guide us in all applications of humility. But that doesn't mean that you should lose yourself in allowing others' light to shine brightly. Jesus didn't lose himself, and his life was not taken, but given of the Father's will and Jesus' faith and obedience to the will of God. He died or gave His life as a human being for the "Greater Good" of humanity but rose as the preeminent King. He died for our mistakes with purpose and Focus in the quadrants of past, present, future and the unknown.

I have made my share of mistakes, but none so great that they should cause others to treat me as if I didn't exist. Not even God treated mankind this way. Humility has it's place, and it goes beyond city limits, for it travels a long way. However, abuse should always be placed on a tight leash of zero tolerance. So, in that your light is dimmed to make others shine, I support that to a point — let not your light be extinguished, however, for the sake of others' ego. You should boldly draw a line in the sand when approaching that outer limit.

Unconditional trust in one's own instinct and having the faith to believe that what is felt in spirit is what the infinite has spoken, and it is requisite to follow the guidance of spirit as opposed to following the advice of wounded people pretending to be healed and whole: in other words, "thrown together."

Unconditional faith is having the confidence and belief that life unfolds as it should, and the infinite is the source of all that is. Those are the ones who will respect, support, and encourage the stance taken to rely on God as your source. It is true that there can be experiences that are similar in nature, but it is not automatic that either experience should have the same result. Of course, it will be scary, and sometimes you will feel lonely, but it is a road less traveled for a reason. It takes a great deal of courage to live to the extent of one's total truth. I am still learning all of who I am, and I am grateful for the soul that abides within me — A soul of integrity. A soul of raw honesty. A soul of pure intention. A soul of genuineness. A soul of loyalty. A soul of humor. A soul of love. I am an individuated expression of God, and I radiate love.

AS A DIVINE PRESENCE

I am full of grace.

I am a servant to fellow beings.

AS A HUMAN BEING

I am forgiving. I am safe and my nature is protective.

I am not entangled in the yokes of depression.

I am free in my spirit because that is my choice and my decision.

Whomsoever God sets free is free indeed.

AS A WOMAN

My presence peacefully shifts the atmosphere.

I am sensual and soft. Nurturing and gentle.

I am radiant as the sun, and my personality is fluid and colorful.

Self-Check

What does the faded reflection in your mirror tell you about yourself?

_____

_____

_____

_____

_____

_____

What patterns no longer serve you in your life?

_____

_____

_____

_____

_____

_____

_____

2 unKonditional
HEARTBREAK-SUFFERING-GRIEF

Unveiling one's heart before the threat of hurt is horrifying, but life is perplexingly enriched by risk.

I remember mamma was sitting on the sofa under a lamp that lit our living room that night. She was reading something in the paper; I don't recall what. My older brother, my mom, and I lived in that three-bedroom apartment on Hollywood Road in Atlanta for as long as I could remember. I had been sitting outside on the front porch with friends; I don't even remember who. She called for me to come inside because it was time for me to get ready for bed and school the next day. As she sat on that sofa wearing her pink sweatsuit, I kissed her on the left cheek and told her good night. My brother wasn't home that night. Little did I know that would be the last chance I would ever have to kiss her again. I remember little else about that night.

The next morning about 7 AM, three days before my fourteenth birthday, my life changed forever. I remember jumping out of bed thinking I was going to be late for school. I still remember parts of the dream I was having when I awoke and rushed to the bathroom across the hallway.

The door was slightly opened. Thinking nothing of it, I pushed the door open and found my mother face down on the floor and non-responsive. I can only imagine that she had fallen in pain, perhaps gasping for air as she landed between the commode and bathtub. Shock, fear, alarm, and confusion consumed me instantly. Terrified, I called out, "Mamma!" She didn't move. I poked at her side and called again, "Mamma! But she didn't answer. I didn't have a clue what to do to help her. My mind was racing, and soon after, panic set in. Now engulfed in immense fear and shock, I ran and sat on the front porch, trying to figure out what to do. Hard to decipher what was going through my mind in those moments on that porch, I remember a guy in the neighborhood who's name I don't even recall, walked by and made a joke that my mom had put me out. Not even responding to him, I rushed back into the house to get my phone. It was a blue and white phone that I kept in my bedroom. I remember tugging on the entangled cord that was stuck on something. After a few forceful yanks, the cord broke free, and I could take it back to the front door where I called my sister.

I vaguely remember knowing her phone number, but somehow it came to me, and I placed the call. When she answered, I just remember saying, "Somethin' wrong with mamma! She in the bathroom on the floor and she not moving!" I would imagine that put her in a nervous panic. She told me to call 911. Why hadn't I thought to call 911? That thought never crossed my mind. Maybe it was wishful thinking that the gravity of the situation wasn't life threatening, something I was not prepared for. So many thoughts rushed in and out in that moment. I called for an ambulance, and I remember the operator was trying to ask me questions to assess the situation, but in my fear and frustration, I just yelled into the phone — "I don't know! Just get here," and I hung up the phone.

The next few moments are black in my mind. The only emotion I can attach to that day is fear. I cannot speak to anything else I was doing or thinking. The ambulance got there, and I directed them to the back where her motionless body lay. While they were in the back, my daddy, showed up. I could only imagine at the time that it was my sister who called him to come see about mamma and me, having instructed me to dial 911 while I was the only one there with her. By that time, the neighbors were all outside.

I can remember my best friend, at the time, walking up the hill, face streaming with tears and asking me, "What's wrong?!"

Drowning in a sea of tears myself, all I could say was, "I don't know — something wrong with mamma."The paramedics brought my mother out on a stretcher; I vividly remember her shirt being open and her breasts visible, but I don't know if her eyes were open or closed. "Why didn't they cover her up?" I remember thinking that as they carried her to the ambulance.

Years later, a friend said to me that she felt like my mom was already dead when they brought her out of the apartment. That moment still flashes in my mind. Feelings of unquenchable fear of that experience is permanently etched in my mind. Nobody knew the pain I felt; I don't even know. Blocked and buried somewhere deep in my subconscious, it has taken me years to admit to myself that I suffered emotional trauma as a child, and, still, sometimes I hesitate to say it because, in my mind, I am supposed to be the strong one. Undoubtedly, something irreversibly traumatic happened to me on that tragically fatal day to both of us; Mamma lost her life and I, barely a teen, lost my lifeline and my protector.

Until that point, she was the entire world to me. I was always with my mamma. Either we were going to church or choir rehearsal, or just going to see about my grandmama. Wherever she went, I went. I can remember many days grandma would call mamma for something even if she needed a stick of butter. Mamma would stop whatever she was doing and go see about her. My grandma lived about forty minutes away, but distance was not a concern for mamma with seeing about grandma. She even had certain days of the month she would dedicate to take grandma around, handling her bills and whatever kind of business she needed to attend to. She taught me how to treat and take care of family. I watched and helped her countless times take care of my grandma. What would she do now?

A beautiful soul, mamma had. Selfless. Loving. She had a quiet strength about her. She didn't have to boast or brag about who she was. Anybody who knew her knew she wasn't with playing games. So strong, but I imagine she still experienced her own heartbreak as most women have. I never got to know that side of her. I often wonder what she must have felt, not as a mother, sister, or daughter, but what she felt as a woman. What did she think? How did she view life? So many unanswered questions. I know she was a woman of many strengths with a witty sense of humor.

I remember being a little girl and going to church, and our car had broken down on the interstate. Somehow she steered that car to the side of the road, but there was this huge metal piece that had come apart from the car that still lay in the middle of the highway. I remember standing in awe, waiting and watching as she risked her life to run out in gaps of traffic to pull whatever that was out of the road. What strength and integrity she had to show concern for us and the safety of oncoming traffic that day. Standing on the side of the road watching her daring efforts to protect the lives of others, risking her own, sealed it for me from that day forth; She became my hero. In that moment, She seemed larger than life. She was no doubt a no-nonsense kind of person, maybe even somewhat abrasive, but all who knew her knew that her love was genuine. A giving heart, she was the one people called on when they were in any trouble. Mamma could cook — I mean really cook — she could've been a baker. I mean, she could bake cakes like nobody's business. One school year, I gave her a list of my classmates, and she baked a cake for each one of them and delivered it to them at school on their exact birthday! Amazingly kind heart! She was the one who taught me how to show up for others, a stern yet gentle soul, now gone.

That moment of her being taken away from that apartment, from me, from my daddy, and from my siblings was surreal. My sister wasn't there and big brother was still away from home, so it was just my daddy and me. They collapsed the legs on the stretcher sliding her in the back of that ambulance, and I got in the truck with my daddy.

In his little blue pickup truck, we followed the ambulance to Grady Memorial Hospital. To this day, I get so anxious that I cannot ride behind an ambulance without experiencing shortness of breath and feeling my chest tighten. I prayed and prayed and begged and prayed, asking God to save my mamma and to let her be okay the entire way to the hospital. I can't imagine what was going through my daddy's mind. Those emotions had to have hit double hard for him. Unbeknownst and dreadfully confusing to me, it was God's will that the soul I had known as mamma no longer had purpose or life on this earth. God had taken her away.

I remember standing in the hallway of a busy emergency room feeling lost and anxiously looking around for a doctor to find out where my mamma was. In constant prayer pleading with God to let her live and that his will be done. Then a doctor came out from I don't know where and said we need to take you to this room and talk to you. I knew then she had died, and I can't even describe to you the adrenaline rush that came over me. But, into this small chapel like room we went, and the doctor was explaining something and even though I knew it, I still needed for him to say it. So, I asked, "Is she ... ?" And he replied, shaking his head, yes. And just like that, my entire world changed. My lifeline clipped — GONE! And I guess, somehow, God expected me to understand.

At that moment I don't know what I felt, but I remember saying, "I wanna go with my mamma." I didn't want to be here without her. What was I going to do without my mamma? Who was going to take care of me?

The doctor came and kneeled to get eye to eye with me, and in a nurturing tone saying to me, "Your mother would not want that. She would want you to continue living your life." Scared, confused and heart stricken, his words brought little comfort. It devastated me. It was as if someone had knocked the breath out of me and I could not catch it, frozen solid in sadness, but hot like immersed in spa water, trapped in a sauna.

I can only wonder what my daddy felt at that moment. Pretty sure it was difficult for him to see his child in such sudden and unthinkable misery, knowing there was nothing he could do. Losing her must have been difficult for him as well. Whatever issues they had or reason they couldn't share a life together, I am sure he loved her, and his heart hurt just like mine.

Shortly after that, my sister came into the room, and before she could say anything, I looked up at her and said, "She gone." She just fell back in the chair and cried and cried. I remember none of the events that followed that moment other than later that evening, my sister telling me I was going home with her.

i. Unanswered Prayer

God didn't answer my prayer, or did he? I can't fathom how He answered my prayer in any shape or form except when I prayed, I said His will be done. He didn't save my mamma, so it must have been that it was God's will that it was time for her lease on life to end. So how does a thirteen going on fourteen-year-old girl move forward feeling like God didn't answer her prayer? She reconciled in her mind either God must not like her, or God does not hear her. Either way, I have carried that thought every day of my life. He could not have heard that little girl in me because he didn't save her mother. So, with nothing else to say, she picked up the pieces and figured out life as best she knew how with those thoughts, feelings, scars and unanswered questions lingering in the back of her mind. And so I struggle through those scars today still.

A truth I never shared with anyone, I wondered if it was my fault mamma died that morning because I froze in fear. I think I punished myself for it. Did I let her die on that bathroom floor because I didn't know what to do and panicked, stricken with fear? My mother's life was in my hands, and I believe that I failed her. So maybe I didn't deserve love, was that my punishment? I'm telling you, I have spent my life trying to win God's approval and keep him from being mad at me. Precariously, I, to this day, am not so sure I wasn't mad at Him.

Somehow, some way, I coped but still never experiencing or expressing the depth of the pain of my greatest loss, my greatest trial. The thought of having to relive that experience terrifies me. I have blocked out spans of time in my mind because the wounded waters are too deep and treacherous to dive. What did I do with that pain, and what did I do with those memories? Where are they in my subconscious? Am I holding that fear in my body somewhere?

The body has a fear response. And now, thirty years later, I still cannot remember, but I fear those emotions. I thought I was fine and had peace with it, but as the days and years continue to pass, I wonder if I properly dealt with those emotions like I should have. What does it even mean to deal with emotions because their not physical, or are they?

It is possible that I am holding them somewhere, but I don't know where or even if I want to know. I don't know how bad it is, but I know it terrifies me to think that I might have to relive the pain of that dreadful day in my life. I am terrified of having to relive that painful day alone, but it may just be something that I must do alone because I did it alone all those years ago. Not a day goes by that I don't think about mamma. I miss her deeply, but I was forced to adjust to life without her. I did that just fine, thanks to my sister, and I am eternally grateful that she sacrificed and kept life as normal as possible for me.

She, like my mother, is selfless in how she shows up for people. Like mamma, she too has taught me to give of myself and show up for the people who mean the most. They bred a sacrificial love into my very core, an unparalleled love, agape: the unconditional, supernatural love that our Heavenly Father has for us. I recognize that it took great strength, love, and an act of faith to take in another child unexpectedly, but she did it with grace and humility. I lived a very normal teenage and early adult life. Like any other teenager, I had my share of issues, but I would like to believe that I was not too much of a burden and certainly not unruly.

It wasn't until later in life that I realised I had been carrying around a burden in my spirit. In my mid to late twenties, I was a risk taker, unafraid to take chances to become successful. I had an interest in real-estate and wanted to own property, so I partnered with a guy whom I thought to be like a brother to me and blindly followed his lead buying my first investment property. Hmn — That was my last.

It didn't "pan out," because I failed to "plan out" to the end. I threw caution to the wind, skipping due diligence of processing "what if" scenarios and jumped in head first, apparently with my trust anchored in the wrong person. The stress, strain, and price tag of trying to rehab and maintain that money pit of an investment property became too much to bear. My business partner had vanished. He stopped answering my phone calls, emails, and texts. I haven't seen him now for some twenty years as of 2021.

I had my dearest brother, who called me "Baby Girl," to lean on. He too is selfless in the way he loves and shows up for me. I am truly grateful for him as I am for my big sister. He stood by me no matter what, and he would help me as much as he could with any and everything, but after a while, I accepted defeat and realised it was time to let the money suctioning property go. I had fallen headlong into a money pit, sustaining a concussion that suppressed my ability to claw my way out. No longer able to sustain financially, I filed for bankruptcy. I say that as if bankruptcy is a bad thing, but I wish that I could become a master of financial investments carrying bankruptcy in my toolbox of great success. Yeah, I know, bankruptcy carries the stigma of apparent failure, but I now realise that it can be legally used for protection and potentially great gain as well.

My lack of diligent planning and blindly placing my trust in someone who may not have deserved my partnership as far as I could tell, led me into a sinkhole without a lifeline. I haven't a clue as to what happened to or with my business partner. He simply went off grid without a trace, dead or alive. That situation stole my zest for life and my desire to step outside the box into my greatness. I have not attempted to try any new ventures since.

That situation left me hopeless of ever achieving my desires, my dreams. Disappointed, regretful, depressed and financially stressed from the demand and failure of that debacle, I decided to go to see a therapist.

ii. After Effects of Trauma

So, I'm sitting in the Therapist's office thinking I'm going to get some needed help with coping because this fool done stressed me out. I took no responsibility in my action and inaction, a planned failure given that I failed to plan. This venture would lead me to learn how to handle stress in my life. I wasn't even thinking that a therapy session had the potential to uncover all kinds of underlying issues that could derail me, upset me even more deeply. But I wasn't worried because I had no other issues in my life that were pressing or hindering me, right?

Well, she asked me to share events of my childhood. So, I did just that then led into the story of the soured investment, which was the primary reason I was there. Why was she even asking me about my childhood, I am here to talk about this fool? It was this conversation that brought about an unwarranted shift for me. While talking to the therapist, I made the comment that the partner I had trusted had just up and left me without a word.

The therapist then said to me, "Well it sounds as though you have abandonment issues."

Surprised and appalled that she would even make such a statement, I rhetorically asked, "Well, Lord, who in the world left me?"

Clueless of the answer to that question, she responded, "Baby, your mother left you."

In shock and awe, "WHAT?!" — "Whaaat?!" She could have knocked me over with a feather.

That thought made me feel uneasy for sure, as I had never even considered that to be a factor for me. I adjusted well in life, or so I thought. Confused and dismayed, I left her office that day swearing to myself that it was not a road that I wanted to re-travel. I was doing fine in my life. There was no need for me to be dredging up any extra issues. But that thought haunted me for years, I just didn't have the courage to face it. I held guilt or blame for myself because I didn't know what to do at that moment. It would be years before I would go back to see that therapist. That was the first time in my life I had ever even heard of having any issues of abandonment.

Hindsight is 20/20. Abandonment has been the common theme in many of my relationships. Everybody somehow would just up and leave, or was I systematically pushing them away because in my mind, I was protecting myself from being hurt? It was both that cultivated the complex individual I have become today. Looking back revealed that tragic experiences which I endured taught me how to disconnect. Because a lot of that time has grayed out in my mind, I imagine I spent a lot of lonely and fearful days wondering why I was having to live through it all.

"Why did my mother have to die?" A question I often ask.

iii. Risk Assessment and Management

I feel cheated to have had to live most of my life without her. Having to unlearn and release that spirit of disconnect has not been easy. Unveiling one's heart before the threat of hurt is horrifying, but life is perplexingly enriched by risk. One never reaches their fullest potential without having taken risk. For some odd reason, the Creator designed life in this fashion. But we must realise that risk is a broad term, so we should understand at a veneer or surface level what that means and the importance of Risk Assessment and Management. Risk, bewilderingly, is inherent to life, defined as an act involving potential danger or loss of something, i.e. money, life, relationships, property and even sanity, but also harmless things such as a friendly game of chess. Although life and risk are inseparable, the many types and facets of risk carry gradients of manageability. We could attempt to sum up the types of risk in the following categories;

- Unsolicited or imposed by others.
- Solicited or Self-imposed.
- Financial or Monetary - investment in stocks, property.
- Injurious or Harmless - physical, mental, reputation.
- Life Threatening or Health - Fatal or debilitating.
- Catastrophic - Epidemic or Pandemic involving many lives localized or global.
- Calculated - weighing the risk carefully based on circumstances, placing value in the least likely probability of danger and the greatest associated gain.

Risk Assessment and Management is key. If we do not assess the risk, we're more likely to fall prey to the attached danger because we cannot manage what we are ignorant of — the unknown or the lack of due diligence to canvass the possible downsides along with potential gain. So risk taking and exposure is inevitable, but manageable to a degree, and we term that calculated risk. Therefore if everything we do is infused with risk, why not take the one that's calculated. For as long as we have breath in our bodies, we are a walking target for risk whether we decide to be classified as risk averse or not. It is that it is.

That the state of disconnect disallows the flow of love in or out, makes for a dismal existence. I didn't want to continue living life from that frame of reference. It was time to make some changes, and I had to start with myself, and taking calculated risks had to become strategic for me Resisting heartbreak has been my mode of living. True, there is a void in my heart that hinders me in a lot of ways. While I may never understand "the why" behind all the events of my life, I know and understand that my failures make me no less deserving of love, nor do my accomplishments warrant narcissistic behavior. It is okay to be proud, but in all things, show gratitude. Humility, honesty, and fairness define characteristics of the woman I want to look back at me from that once faded reflection in the mirror. The more I take back my power, the clearer that faded reflection becomes. I understand there are pieces of me that may never heal. One never gets over the loss of a parent, but they learn to live in-spite of the pain. It is okay to feel sadness, but the key is to try not to remain stagnant in sadness. So I'm aware of the nature of risk, and therefore I am able to manage it while in this body because risk doesn't die until you breathe your last breath. Only then are the two separable.

Day by day, those who have experienced great pain learn to adjust to a new normal. Traumatic loss has the propensity to change a person drastically. The change may neither manifest as good or bad, in which case, it just is. But the impact could be far reaching either way. We need a village of people who are willing and able to love us past our pain. There is an eternal hole in my heart, but I cannot let that hole rob me of experiencing genuine love and happiness as God intended. I believe I have an opportunity to do things better than I used to. Unfettered risk versus the preferred calculated risk: Risk aversion compared to likely probability of net gain from assessed risk. I have lived with the pain, the fear, the sadness, but I must not let it define the totality of who I choose to be. I must not allow it to seal me off from life itself, knowing that I am powerful and gaining strength in-spite of risk and because of smart risk engagement.

What I now know about fear is that I must not let it determine my behavior in life. Fear is a prohibitor of all things. To experience the fullness of life, one must learn how to keep moving within fear and risk taking. For it does not go away, the individual must learn how to set it aside to accomplish goals and dreams. I have allowed pause in my life because of the fear of forward movement and the catastrophic failure of risk taking. It is there, but we must implement risk assessment and manage it, not allow it to consume and strangle us. It keeps us from reaching felicity, the "happily ever after" we seek.

Self-Check

What trauma left you in a place of resting heartbreak?

_____

_____

_____

_____

_____

_____

_____

Does fear immobilize you in certain areas of your life? If so, how?

_____

_____

_____

_____

_____

_____

_____

3 unKonditional FAITH

The belief that all things are possible insinuates a need for ... Faith without limit.

Hebrews 11:1 Now faith is the substance of things hoped for the evidence of things not seen. (NKJV) Restated:

Now belief in God is the essence of things hoped for, the proof of things not visible. It's important to realise that this is not the definition of faith, rather a product or action caused by faith. Let's restate this as a literal translation of the translation which includes the definitions of faith, substance and evidence.

Your unwavering belief in the power and promise of God (Faith) causes you to in essence (substance) hope for something, completely trusting that it has been or will be manifested (evidenced) even though there is no tangible proof (evidence) that the thing desired has been granted.

The word faith derives from the Greek word pistis and it means belief, firm persuasion, assurance, or firm confirmation. Faith is believing that no matter what the situation may be, God is working it out. The belief in limitations puts a definite strain on the miracles performed in one's life.

Putting limitations on thinking puts limitations on God's ability. Limiting God keeps the essence of his omnipotence in a box. God is not a conditioned consciousness, not to be held to conditional standards. God is infinite: so are the possibilities. He exists outside of that which He created, space, matter, and time. It is imperative to have faith that the infinite source of our being has our best interest in mind. In my estimation, there would be little glory for God if everyone's blessing manifested in the same way.

God created us to heal and serve each other, self-evolve, and to give all praise and glory to Him. No two people are blessed in exactly the same way, nor reach a place of healing and wholeness precisely the same. Each individual shares a personal relationship with God and so will be delivered from their transgressions in the way that God uniquely sees fit for the particular individual, just as each person has a unique fingerprint. There is no credence in the expectation of God to interact with healing power or deliverance of a person in the same way as anyone else. God is not redundant in the sense that everything in the universe is homogeneous. Blessings or healing will not present the same face. One look at the universe and all its intricacies will dispel that notion. Heightened energetic vibrations of an individual influences heightened awareness of the Highest Good for themselves and others. The point of humanity is to see everyone reach the highest potential possible.

Love is universal and a common goal for all, and faith should be the basis of belief for everything. The belief that all things are possible insinuates a need for unconditional faith. Faith without limit. Faith to believe when nothing seems, looks, or feels like it's right. Faith to trust when things do not go as planned: the premise of unconditional faith. I think all people have in some way or another placed limits on their faith, only believing their level of understanding. For many people, faith is believing in what they can see. The thought of believing beyond what we see with the naked eye is not common. It was hard for me to wrap my mind around the concept of believing anything was possible when nothing looked right. Yes, I grew up in church, but I limited my faith. I believe in God, but I only believed in what I could see manifested. It was difficult for me to put my trust in things that were not visible. The hardest thing would be the relinquishing of control and allowing space to believe and trust in the uncertainties of life. The unknown terrifies us the most. We all are creatures of habit, and embracing anything that is beyond one's comfort zone is threatening.

Unconditional trust is having the ability to remain calm and be confident when everything seems to go wrong and having the ability to trust when one does not understand. That is not the easiest thing to do. God will always send the answers that are being sought in His time, not necessarily the time you specify. Hearing that still small voice is a matter of training and opening oneself to receive the answer, and I don't believe this is literal. It is a matter of being receptive to hearing and honoring what resonates in the spirit. God, in all his mastery, can and will speak in ways that one can understand, but not necessarily audibly in my experience. The confirmation will soon follow specific messages needed for one to understand. Confirmations come in several ways, so the individual must be open to receive and willing to hear what is being said, even if what is being said is a message that the individual is not yet ready to receive. The mistake that most people make is thinking that God is going to speak audibly and behave the same as with everyone else. That was the mistake I made. I kept waiting for this voice to whisper in my ear but was always being told God will not speak in his voice. Their explanations confused me even more and made things worse. No one I asked could make it make sense for me. And because I was desperate to literally hear the voice of God, I relied on my spirit communicating with the Holy Spirit within me to make it make sense for me, but I found that God does not whisper.

One thing I learned is that most people touting that God speaks in this literal still small voice were not sure themselves, and that is why they could not help me understand. I subscribe to people who can tell me with confidence about their experience and imperfections in their faith. For me, that is real, believable, respectable. I grew exhausted, subscribing to so-called perfect Christians who only passed down ridicule and judgment along with their practiced tales. I wanted to tap into what was real and what made sense for me. My soul was craving it. Yes, sometimes I am still unsure, but the insecurity is because of my own misunderstanding, I'm sure. I'm learning to trust that God will lead, though. But what we should realise is that God left us with His instructional word, His manual to govern our lives, and it requires our in depth study and prayer to understand that which we cannot decipher that unveils His truth, His guidance. In those moments of intense, fervent prayer and seeking of Him, I lean on what resonates in my spirit the strongest.

I put my confidence in listening to my body and my soul. I tested it. When something was not right, my body felt uneasy. So, I learned to listen to that. Not sure if that is right, but it feels right for me at my level of understanding. Again, my experience has been that God does not whisper in a still small voice, and that has no reflection on accounts of the Scripture of stories in the old testament where he spoke to Moses, Samuel, Elijah, Elisha and other prophets. It does not disturb my belief that some were led by God by putting out a fleece in the Old Testament when there was no Bible at all to follow. But scripture does not support what some may purport. When the time comes for me to change, then I will, but under God's command and not the command of man. I started trusting that it was God's way of speaking to me when thoughts or ideas just dawned on me or when they came to me as if they just sprung into my head with no link or apparent origin. I paid attention to how the messages would come in. One could miss the message if they are looking at someone else's revelation or breakthrough. I learned that I would not find my miracle hidden within the shell of someone else's breakthrough. That assumes limits on God's capability. As finite beings, we must clear our minds of clutter and open ourselves to receive, and where we are unsure of how to open that door, we should pray fervently that God will accept our complete submission to His guidance to remove any barricades to receiving.

Faith is having the ability to surrender completely to the infinite and being able to rest in what one knows in their soul to be true. Changing the narrative, I told myself my entire life was nothing shy of difficult. That battle in my head and heart is tiring, and I need to work harder to change that for myself. I often hesitate in prayer because there is still that fear that God does not hear me. Then sometimes I am so overwhelmed with my thoughts and emotions, it is hard to muster up the words to even try to pray. My heart was broken so much so that I stopped trusting God with my heart. I didn't believe that he would take care of it because he kept allowing it to be crushed. But I must be accountable for my participation in those situations. I am learning to release that worry and surrender to the divine and trust that He sees my best interest as first and foremost. I don't understand it at all, but placing my trust in anything other than God is never an option. What is clear to me, though, is that I have to get my weight up with a diet of healthy meals of trust, faith, healing and total submission.

Trust equates to rest. Let God and rest. The removal of a need to control and manipulate a situation is rest. Resting in whatever God sees fit and finding the courage to find a peaceful mindset in the midst of a storm. One must learn to surrender the need to control, take a hands off approach to the situation, and be still. As I minister these words to you, I minister them to myself. What does it mean to be still?

Being still means to not focus on the situation, to not try to fix it according to the wants of the individual. We say we are going to give a situation to God, but then we take it back. Guilty of that myself. God will not override one's free will, if one thinks they can fix it better. I believe God will allow us to attempt just what we believe, even if it means failure. God knows that in time we will come back asking for help, and He will always be patiently waiting with open arms. There may be a bit of chastening for those He loves, but He is always near.

We must learn to let God be God and allow him to move as he sees fit. It is a hard task, because somewhere along the way, we taught ourselves that we can handle things, God is too slow, or He will not handle it the way we want. Yep, that's what we tell ourselves. The need to control things comes from fear of disappointment. People believe that their control of a situation will lessen the chances of being disappointed. Sometimes the hardest thing to do is let go. We want what we want, but sometimes the things we want are not the best, or it is just not the right time.

Unconditional faith is also trusting in divine timing. We establish a personal relationship with God in daily communion spirit to Spirit, trusting in God's guidance. God understands and knows how to meet everyone just where they are. He can get the attention, time, commitment and dependency of the individual that He desires, even if it means chastening to achieve a submissive spirit within the individual just so he can shape you for the blessing he has for you. People on the outside will not understand and often-times will talk a person out of what they already know to be true in their heart. So, it is crucial not to contaminate the connection to source with outside influence. They will talk you out of your healing and blessing, because your faith isn't strong enough to acknowledge that God is infinite and heals according to what is necessary to get one to a place of wholeness. One must follow instinctive intuition. The divine creator will lead no one astray. We must not allow other people to dictate the decisions that have been chosen for oneself. When we allow others to dictate our path, we allow them to become god over our lives and circumstances.

The belief in God and fellowship, going to church, is the foundation of my faith. I started singing in the choir very young. It was the best thing ever to stand alongside my cousins and sing songs that now have so much meaning, songs that I didn't quite understand then. It is true, it takes a village. I am humbled that there was a village to keep me in church after mamma died. My cousin, Cookie, would come and take me to choir rehearsals and church. She did her best to keep that part of my life as normal as possible. I learned to appreciate and honor God through song. It set the foundation that there was a higher power that I could go to and grow to. Church is where I learned to feel God's presence. Without fail, when I got up to sing, midway through the song, I would always cry. I didn't understand what that meant then. I have concluded that that was God's presence. It was my soul crying out in honor of God's grace. Those words had significant meaning. They pierce the soul. God has always been an unconditional presence in my life, even when I didn't understand.

I spent a lot of time singing in that choir stand with my cousins. Looking back, I realise time is sacred and special. It taught me how to connect in faith with others. Even in those moments when I told myself that God does not hear me, there was a part of me that knew differently. There is restoration in those songs. They bring peace and soothe uneasy souls.

I had lost my faith that God hears me in those moments after mamma died, and, still, in a lot of instances, I struggle with that thought. That is the story I told myself, and the attempt to change the narrative that I held in my head has been nothing short of difficult, but every day I put forth an effort to change that narrative. God has never let me down, but not everything has gone my way in life. That is where my true faith lives. A small grain of faith that kept me grounded even when the outcome was not what I wanted or expected. Faith and acceptance that God is in control gave me the power to rest in those dark moments of misunderstanding. To find peace and accept those conditions when they were not favorable was what I needed to do. My character matured, and I birthed my boundaries. A deeper love for myself emerged, and I realised I didn't have to endure abuse to experience love. Love should never feel like abuse in any language. It had been so long since I felt love that I didn't know how to accept it when it showed up; I didn't trust or believe it was real.

I didn't believe God listened to me, and the disappointed me is on record with God, saying, "You took my mamma, why won't you give me this?" How dare I try to manipulate God, using my grief to barter for what I wanted! That was wrong and quite selfish of me.

Unconditional Faith has taught me, though, that God has never left me. He has always shown up when I asked for help, even when I didn't deserve it. I just have a hard time asking. Losing mamma was just a part of my journey, and as far as I can remember, I didn't question it too much. I just accepted it. The little thirteen-year-old girl in me will never understand why her mamma had to go or why she had to be the one to find her, but it has given the grown up me a strength that I cannot explain. Losing her taught me self-sufficiency. The pain of that day was profound, and I think I blocked it out for my own survival. I would have loved to have spent my days with her, but that was not the path my soul was destined for. Losing her has taught me to appreciate mothers, and it enlightens in that they were women before they were mothers. I wish I could have known the extraordinary woman that was my mother, my friend, my protector.

For me, unconditional faith is about trust. Trust that God will provide. Without a mother, God will provide. No matter the need, God is the source of all that is and will ever be. It is always best to learn to follow and trust God for yourself. We all have an innate ability to know the answers if we learn to be still and listen. To be perfectly honest with you, that is still sometimes a struggle, but that motivates me to seek oneness with the Spirit within me.

I didn't know how to stretch past what I could see and believe in, what I could not see, nor how to go beyond my level of understanding. All things are possible means that my healing, blessings and deliverance will manifest from an infinity pool, but in a sense finite within the moral will of God. I spent too much time expecting things to happen in ways that look and feel familiar or normal, and when they didn't, it became customary to dismiss any other possibility. I had to understand that God made everyone different, having unique characteristics to create distinct personalities and talents. Although healing is universal, my healing pattern would not necessarily mimic someone else's pattern. My healing will be specific to my journey, and someone else's healing will be specific to the experiences from which they need healing on their life journey.

As I began listening to my own soul, that became quite clear to me. Granted, I could not believe because I had never even opened my mind to accept that level of truth, but the more I fought for my own individuality, the more I was enlightened. It resonated a truth within me I could not deny. I learned more about that truth, and even in my disbelief, I had to remind myself of those words. Re-conditioning my own thoughts to believe that God is infinite, and my healing is tailored to my journey. We don't have the same experiences, nor are we bruised in the same places, so why expect the pattern of healing to look the same?

Being open to the notion that things are not always going to look or manifest the way we think they should, I had to learn to have unconditional faith that my creator has the infinite intelligence to bring me to the appointed place of my destined greatness at the appointed time. I may not know what to do, but as long as I show a willingness to trust and follow what I feel is God's lead, I believe it will all work out somehow. Even if I make a wrong decision, God has the power to bring me full circle to where I need to be. I understand now that I should not worry so much on "the how" and place my trust in the Infinite Source that created all the universe. I just need to learn to allow myself to be led. God will get me to where I need to be when I need to be there, but I must be a vessel to his plan, and therefore I must plan according to His desires for me. It will never be easy, but it is very much possible.

I have learned to stop trying to force things, creating friction, rather live on a path of least resistance. That was and is the hardest thing to accept. No matter how I tried to discredit and turn away from my knowing, it never left my consciousness. Getting caught up in the lie I was selling myself to keep from being hurt was easy. The mask was overdue for elimination. Depending on people was not comfortable for me, so I was depending on myself because people often let me down. I gave myself permission to take off the mask and be alright with what I felt without being judged for it. I opened up about my truth, embraced it and felt great not judging myself for it. Living life through the fabricated narrative I was selling to myself prevented me from reaching any level of healing. Wearing that mask to prove my strength to everyone else was true to a certain extent, though. While I was strong, there were times I needed to be taken care of. I yearned for reciprocity.

It is not always good to share vulnerabilities with others deemed close to you. Where those vulnerabilities may become tools to dismantle a person, it proves beneficial to be selective in who one opens their soul to. Being lost in what I thought other people thought, it was clear I needed to trust myself realizing that my vulnerabilities and their existence made me no less deserving of love and respect. Still not free from my insecurities or fears, my faith grew stronger in my willingness to show my vulnerabilities to the trusted ones who have proven no ill intent. Otherwise, I remained guarded to those with whom I viewed would have the propensity to use my vulnerabilities as ammunition against me on a whim of selfishness.

Unconditional faith will influence discernment to feel the energized vibes of those with whom we come in contact. Faith is universal, and I accept and believe that there is truth all around in all disciplines and philosophies as it pertains to faith. As I embrace spirituality and open myself to divine truth, my faith leads me to want to understand a universal truth. I appreciate and respect the truth in all disciplines or schools of thought. I am not claiming to be an expert on any one religion or discipline, but from that which I have read and understand, I believe the common theme is to treat people well and to have a heart of service toward your fellow human beings.

Evvverything in life seems connected to how we treat one another, the ecosystem of life and existence, perhaps. I think it embodies a powerful level of humility. There are so many truths out there, and everybody swears their way is the right way, but how can one be so sure? We don't know. All we can do is have faith that God see's the grace and humility in one's heart. To say that one religion, spiritual practice, or faith is right over another seems to be a construct of the ego. The ego is always at play. If it honors God, why does it get pummeled with jeers instead of lauded with cheers? Who made your religion or worship right and another's wrong? That's what I often ask myself. Truth of it is that I don't have all the answers, and neither do you, and all that we can be sure of is we never will. Not in this body, not on this earth. As certain as we are alive, we shall certainly die, no debate on that.

The best I can do is treat all people, including myself, with kindness and know that God sees the pure intentions of my heart. In pursuit of our Highest Good, all God wants us to do is love. There are some that will bombard you with all kinds of history to prove their point, but who's to say? Don't misunderstand me, for The Focus Quadrants is incomplete without history, obviously. But it is the twist that some place on historical events that can be misleading whether through omission or commission. How dare anyone think their thought process or belief is better or more correct than someone else's. Here again, ego in full effect. Having faith is about having respect. I, for one, think God honors pure intentions and actions of a person more so than whether they practice a specific religion or spiritual practice. According to God, I cannot be wrong, because for me, it's about love of God — humility — love of self — respect — love of humanity — love for love — love returned for hatred. Respect is having the ability to give others the space to believe what they believe without shunning their soul to hell. People are so quick to put others in hell when the truth of the matter is, none of us have a clue nor heaven to promote nor hell to relegate someone or authority to sanction either. Just who do we think we are?

While God uses us as vessels to bring souls to Him, we are not His henchmen, judges, nor angels to slaughter, condemn, nor crown. So we would do well to love, respect another person's journey, and ultimately allow God the Father to touch the heart, convert and save or do whatever it is that He does. Only God can save, heal, transform or effect final judgment. So, it's a matter of letting your light shine, sharing the God you serve with those in need, then support, getting out of the way and letting God be God. I believe there is truth in all religious beliefs and so, I respect whatever someone believes, even if it is different from my own.

i. Christianity

Christianity is a monotheistic faith of holy trinity: God (the father), Christ (the son) and the Holy Spirit. Although the holy trinity is not a term used in the original manuscripts, nor any bible today, we see evidence of a triune God especially in the New Testament. In Israel, the Jews were God's chosen people, and their shema pointed to only one God, hence a monotheistic faith.

Deut 6:4 "Hear O Israel, The Lord our God, the Lord is one." (NKJV)

The belief is that God sent his only son to save the world from sin. Subdivided into denominations based on congregational similarities, traits such as name, history, organization, leadership, theological doctrine, and styles of worship. These denominations fraught with dogmas and differing principles vary in degree to the standards in which they identify with each other. Some sects believe they are successors of the church started by Jesus Christ himself and other sects believe in denominationalism, which is where Christians believe all groups or churches are the same regardless of labels.

Hebrews 11:1-3 says that "Now faith is the substance of things hoped for, the evidence of things not seen. For by it, the elders obtained a good report." (NKJV)

Through faith, we understand that the worlds were framed by the word of God so that things which are seen were not made of things which appear. The righteous shall live by faith and grow. The measure of faith, metaphorically compared to the size of a mustard seed, given by God, is believed enough to move any "mountain" or perceived obstacle that hinders forward progression. Put in that small amount of faith and believe that all is possible, and the solid believer is thought to aptly overcome anything. Granted, this is a process that one must work daily to develop but believed to be very much within the realm of possibility under the canopy of Christianity. By faith, we understand that the universe was formed at God's command.

Hebrews 11-6 "And without faith it is impossible to please God, because anyone who comes to him must believe that he exists and that he rewards those who earnestly seek him." (KJV)

Faith reveals the righteousness of God. The just shall live by faith.

Living in faith is key to living a Christian life. Trust and faith are two of the most dangerous things to extend to man. Believers should only give them to Christ. Christianity is built on trust in Christ, for salvation is gained through Christ only. Trust in God for one's own life gives power to stand apart from the crowd to hear and follow spirit, commonly referred to as sanctification translated from the Greek word hagiasmos, meaning a process of being set apart, declared perfect in principle though not yet attained. As aforementioned, the ending of this Greek term, "-asmos," means continual, so the process of perfection is always ongoing and never complete in the flesh.

Faith in Christianity means having faith in its law also known as divine authority, but summed up in the Perfect Law of Liberty as defined by Jesus, the preeminent christ. This law handed down to and through Moses is referred to as the ten commandments. These are universal guiding principles written by God.

John 15:12-14 [12] "This is My commandment, that you love one another as I have loved you. [13] Greater Love has no one than this,

than to lay down one's life for his friends. [14] You are my friends if you do whatever I command you." (NKJV)

John 14:21 "He who has my commandments and keeps them, it is he who loves Me. And he who loves Me will be loved by My Father, and I will love him and manifest Myself to him." (NKJV)

Matt 22:37-40 [37]... You shall love the Lord your God with all your heart, with all your soul, and with all your mind. [38] This is the first and great commandment. [39] And the second is like it: 'You shall love your neighbor as yourself.' [40] On these two commandments hang all the Law and the Prophets." (NKJV)

Mark 12:29-31 [29] "The greatest of all the commandments is: Hear,

O Israel, the Lord our God, the Lord is One. [The Shema, Deuteronomy 6:4]. [30] And you shall love the Lord your God with all your heart, with all your soul, with all your mind, and with all your strength. This is the first commandment. [31] And the second, like it, is this: 'You shall love your neighbor as yourself.' There is no other commandment greater than these." (NKJV)

This illustration of the greatest of the commandments is referred to as the Perfect Law of Liberty constructed from Deut 6:5 and the Royal Law (Lev 19:18), the second of the greatest commandments.

10 Commandments

Thou shalt not covet

Remember the Sabbath and keep it holy

Thou shalt not make unto thee any graven images

Thou shalt not take the name of the Lord thy God in vain

Thou shalt not kill (the greatest injury to a person-murder)

Thou shalt have no other God's before me (to worship only God)

Thou shalt not steal (the greatest injury to movable property—theft)

Thou shalt not commit adultery (the greatest injury to family bonds)

Honor thy father and thy mother (the greatest intergenerational obligation)

Thou shalt not bear false witness against thy neighbor (the greatest injury to commerce and law)

Faith in Christianity is also having a relationship with God. We build a relationship with God through prayer. Prayer is how one communicates with God, the supreme being having many names including YHWH, Yaweh, El Shaddai (Almighty), El Elyon (Most High God), Adonai (Lord & Master), and Elohim (the creator). The Christian faith believes in the Redemptive names of God thus attributed to Jesus:

Jehovah Jireh - The Breasty One who sees my needs, My Provider

Jehovah Tsidkenu - My Righteousness

Jehovah Nissi - My Standard, My Banner, My Victory

Jehovah Shalom - The Lord is Peace

Jehovah Rapha - My Healer

Jehovah Ra'ah - My Shepherd

Jehovah Shammah - the One who never leaves, nor forsakes me

Jehovah M'Kaddesh - The Lord My Sanctifier

Unconditional faith influences prayer with humility, not always asking for the change to occur in other people, but petitioning a change takes place within oneself. Judgments passed on by others are missed opportunities to recognize the flaws within oneself. For it is on the other side of those judgmental moments that one can connect to the God within. Faith and connection to spirit replaces denial with acceptance. It turns chaos into order and confusion into clarity.

Hebrews 6:12 (KJV) "Faith and patience inherit promise."

Faith should always be the focal point of having trust in Adonai, the creator, while leaning not to one's own understanding and in always acknowledging God, and He will direct their path. Faith allows one to live in the comfort of knowing that all will work out. Listening and trusting one's own intuition can often be a struggle, like anything else, it takes time and patience to nurture and grow the faith to block out the crowd to hear the voice of God. The battle in one's own mind is the biggest battle they might face. Of course, faith will sometimes be distant if not obsolete, but unconditional trust will lead the way back to God's unchanging hand. Even through anger and tears, surrender in faith that God hears and answers prayer. The universe by the command of God will always guide the individual to a place of peace and restoration.

God imputes his righteousness to us by His grace, not by our works, and there is no amount of works that we can do to earn the status of being and standing righteous before God. This is exactly what Genesis is referring to as it is referenced by James and Paul, only James throws in the only twist that he shouldn't have: works required for salvation. He does this a bit over-zealously because he is so passionate in addressing the twelve tribes on an issue where they don't seem to be faithful to Royal Love and the Perfect Law of Liberty as Jesus instructed reference the greatest commandment. Christians love to flaunt the mantra, "Faith without works is dead;" derived from James 2:17, and in the proper context, it makes a strong statement about action towards our fellow brethren and walk of love in life as Jesus commanded. Cautiously, I say, though, that the substance that James spins the web with as an argument is not perfectly aligned with the scripture of the old testament. If I could rewrite all that James was attempting to say, I'd do it in this way;

As a bi-product, the fabric of works is spun from the "silk of faith alone" that through God's grace profits the believer justification and therefore salvation. Said another way, that self same "silk of faith alone" which profited the believer with justification and salvation by God's grace should glorifyingly and naturally spin webbed actions of love toward humanity.

James knew that faith alone is all that God requires to justify the believer, but his intent was to address the walk of the justified, honoring the grace that God had bestowed upon he who claimed to be steeped in belief and faith. So, as we acknowledge that inevitable bi-product of faith, there is a call for action characterized by good works rooted in faith. Justification and salvation, requiring no works, no action at all, is wrapped in the fabric of faith alone. But the walk of faith is about action. Action is how one relates caringly and morally to oneself and others. Faith governs how we treat others. Faith is trust and belief in the power of God, period. A common myth is the belief that before one can have faith, they must understand God. As servants we can learn and understand the word of God, but to understand the full essence of the supreme being is impossible. There is no foreseen possibility that one's finite mind can intelligibly comprehend the mind of the infinite. Faith is birthed in the acceptance of that truth. It is a belief and trust in a supreme being or consciousness that holds the best interest of one's soul.

Importantly, Paul's brilliance in the intimate epistle to the Romans stands apart as it clearly and holistically architects the doctrine that faith alone justifies.

Paul makes it clear that no one can boast of works when it comes to righteousness and God's Grace.

Romans 3:28 "Therefore we conclude that a man is justified by faith [APART FROM] the deeds of the law." (NKJV)

Romans 4:2-4 "²For if Abraham were justified by works, he has something to boast about, but not before God. ³For what does the scripture say? 'Abraham believed God and it was accounted to him for righteousness.' ⁴Now to him who works, the wages are not counted as grace but debt." (NKJV)

David celebrated the same truth —

Romans 4:6 "Just as David also describes the blessedness of the man to whom God imputes righteousness apart from works." (NKJV)

Were it for David's deeds to attain righteousness, concerning the atrocity with Bathsheba and Uriah, he would not have lived according to ancient Biblical Law, and presumably, this law was in effect at that time.

Leviticus 20:10 "The man who commits adultery with another man's wife, he who commits adultery with his neighbor's wife, the adulterer and the adulteress, shall be put to death." (NKJV)

Romans 4:13-15 " ¹³ For the promise that he would be the heir of the world was not to Abraham or to his seed through the law, but through the righteousness of faith. ¹⁴ For if those who are of the law are heirs, faith is made void and the promise made of no effect, ¹⁵ because the law brings about wrath; for where there is no law, there is no transgression." (NKJV)

ii. Judaism

Faith in Judaism requires one to honor God through constant struggle with God's instruction in the Torah and the practice of the Mitzvot which are the commandments of God. Believers believed that any disbelief of these principles makes the nonbeliever a heretic, one whose beliefs or opinions are contrary to the collective beliefs of emunah, the faith.

General practice in Judaism is to devote oneself to the study of Torah; observe the laws. Emunah in English is faith or belief. In quite a few instances, it can be more about belief in God as well as trust and reliance on God which predicate consistent behavior. It refers to God's faithfulness, and justice is rendered unto all his people, accurately referring to an innate conviction or perception of truth based on reason, enhanced through wisdom, knowledge, and understanding of Jewish sacred writings. The fundamental text is theorem. Unlike other traditional religions, Judaism does not view skepticism as a second class. Judaism does not require faith statements as a sign of legitimacy. It does not require the believer to give up their questions or to deny their doubt.

According to Judaism, faith is not a starting point of the journey. Maimonides, also known as the Rambam, known as Judaism's greatest medieval philosopher, created what he calls the "shlosha asar ikkarim," the thirteen fundamental principles of the Jewish faith which are a series of faith statements defining Judaism.

Maimonides, Greek for Moses, wrote the Mishneh Torah, which was the first ever comprehensive code of Jewish Law. His family was exiled from Cordoba and it is said that he practiced Islam publicly and Judaism secretly. He outlined the thirteen principles of Jewish belief, which was deemed a controversial undertaking of non-creedal Judaism. He based his teachings on the beliefs that descriptions about God were allegorical. According to Maimonides, these descriptions are "... adapted to the mental capacity of the majority of humans, who recognize only physical bodies." [18]

---

[18] Daniel Septimus. The Thirteen Principles of Faith. 2002 – 2020.
https://www.myjewishlearning.com/article/the-thirteen-principles-of-faith/

The Torah speaks in the language of humanity. "All these phrases are allegorical"[19] Maimonides recognized language is inadequate to describe God who is beyond ordinary human cognition.[20] Judaism, as one of the three monotheistic faiths, is characterized by a belief in one God.

As the Torah showed, it is a program of human action rooted in personal confrontation. Further, the response of this people to its encounter with God is viewed as significant for all humankind. The Jewish community is called to express loyalty to God and the covenant by exhibiting solidarity within its corporate life on every level, including every aspect of human behavior from the most public to the most private.[21]

---

[19] Mishneh Torah, Foundational Laws of the Torah, 1.9, https://www.myjewishlearning.com/article/maimonides-rambam/.

[20] Ibid.

[21] Silberman, Lou Hackett. Judaism. July 20,1998. https://www.britannica.com/topic/Judaism/additional-info#history. Encyclopedia Britannica, Inc. June.2020

The thirteen   principles   of Judaism

Belief in God's eternity

Belief in immutability of the Torah

Belief in the existence of the creator

Belief in the divine origin of the Torah

Belief in God's omniscience and providence

Belief in God's absolute and unparalleled unity

Belief in the primary prophecy of Moses, our teacher

Belief that God communicates with many through prophecy

The imperative to worship God exclusively and no foreign false God's

Belief in God's non-corporeality, nor that he will be affected by any physical occurrences such as movement, rest, dwelling.

Belief in the messiah and the messianic era

Belief in divine reward and retribution

Belief in resurrection of the dead

iii. Islam

In the name of Allah, the Beneficent, the Merciful:

The actual roots of Islam go back further than the 7th century. Scholars have typically dated that period of time as its birth in Mecca, which is now referred to as Saudi-Arabia. Islam is derived from "sal'm", the Arabic word which when translated literally means peace, but Islam, itself, means "submission" in the Arabic language, but when applied in the religious context, it means "submission to the will of God."

Islam is the world's second largest monotheistic faith. Muslims believe that God revealed His divine revelations to Prophet Muhammad (peace be upon him). They believe Allah ta'ala chose many prophets and messengers to teach His word to the people. 25 prophets are mentioned in the Qur'an, whereas many believe that there were 124,000 messengers and prophets altogether. In Islam, the Arabic name for God is Allah, which means "God / The One and Only God," and Allah is not considered a physical creation in any sense or holy statue.

One central idea in Islam is "jihad" which means "struggle," not terrorism. While the term has been viewed negatively in mainstream culture due to some extremist and fear mongering propaganda by media sources, Muslims believe it refers to internal and external efforts to defend their faith. An intimate struggle to purify the soul of satanic influence, or inner struggle of the soul to obey what God has said is good (halal), and it forbids all that is considered evil (haram).

A clear definition of faith serves as the basis for understanding of Islam. In the Arabic language, faith (al-iman) means to affirm something and to comply with it. It is believed that faith is more about affirmation than it is belief. This affirmation also includes behavior and speech that is governed by the heart of a person. Faith in Islam means to believe in Allah, to affirm his truth and submit to his commands. Believing in the six articles of faith is an essential principle of the Islamic belief:

a. Belief in Allah

The Muslim believes in Allah the Most High, I.e. he believes in the existence of the Lord, and that it is He who originated the heavens and the earth, that He knows the seen and the unseen as well. He is the Lord and the Sovereign of all creatures, none has the right to be worshipped except

Him, and there is no true Lord except Him. All of His Attributes are perfect.

He is free of any deficiency whatsoever.[22]

b. Belief in His Angels

The Muslims believes in the angels of Allah the Almighty. He believes that they are among the most honorable and dignified of His creatures. He also believes that Allah created the angels from light as man was created from surrounding clay of the earth like the clay of pottery and that jinns were created from a smokeless flame of fire. He also believes that Allah has assigned specific missions for them to carry out: those who guard the worshippers, those who record their deeds, those assigned to work in Paradise with its favors, and the opposite extreme of the gradient, those assigned to work in the Fire with its chastisement. Some of them spend all day and night without slacking in the glorification of Allah.

The Muslim believes that Allah preferred some of them over others; of them are those who are most favored such as: Jibril, Mika'il, and Israfil.

Others do not necessarily hold the same status.[23]

c. Belief in the Books of Allah

The Muslim believes in all that Allah the Almighty revealed in the Books, and in the scriptures He gave to some of His messengers. All of these revelations are the Word of Allah revealed to His messengers for the purpose

---

[22] Al-Jaza'iry, Abu Bakr Jabir, Lecturer in the Noble Prophetic Masjid, Volume 1: Minhaj Al-Muslim, A Book of Creed, Manners, Character, Acts of Worship and other Deeds, First Edition March 2001, Chapter 1, Creed, pg. 19)

[23] Ibid, pg 43

of conveying His law and religion (to their people). Because of their belief, they accept the Torah (Tawrah) of Moses (may God be pleased with him), the Psalms (Zabur) of "David" (may God be pleased with him) and The Gospel (Injil) of Jesus (may God be pleased with him). Muslims have an unshakable belief that the Noble Qur'an stands as a guardian over all the other Books, a confirmation of the Bible, and it abrogates all the other Books' rules and regulations.[24]

d. Belief in his prophets

The Muslim believes that Allah the Almighty chose Messengers and Prophets from among the people to whom He sent down His legislation. They set the best examples of moral and spiritual conduct. Allah commanded them to convey this revelation so that mankind should have no argument (against Him) on the Day of Judgment. He also sent them with clear proof and supported them with miracles. Nuh (may God be pleased with him) was the first Messenger, and Muhammad (peace be upon him) was last of all prophets and the perfect guidance for all of mankind to follow.

All the Messengers and Proponents were human beings. They suffered from what other men suffer: they ate and drank, were subject to healthiness and illness, forgot and remembered, and lived and died. The were the most perfect of humans and one's faith will not be complete unless and until he believes in all of them.[25]

---

[24] Ibid, pg 48

[25] Ibid, pg 58

e. Belief in the day of judgment

Islam teaches that physical death is not the end of a person's existence. The Muslim believes there will be a Final Hour bringing the end to this worldly life, and that there will be a Last Day after which there will be no other day. Then the Second Life comes. The term "Last Day" refers to events of the Hereafter when Allah, the Almighty, will resurrect all the creatures, gather them before Him and call them all to account for their good and bad deeds. Then He will reward the pious with the eternal bliss in Paradise, and the evildoers with the disgraceful chastisement in the Fire.

Muslims believe the Trumpet will be blown once for all the great terror and annihilation and again for resurrection and gathering to congregate before the Lord of the Worlds. Then the records will be issued; some will receive their records with their right hands and others with their left hands.

Then the Scale (Al-Mizan) will be erected, and Reckoning will begin. This ends with those destined for Paradise entering it and those destined for the Fire entering it. [26]

f. Belief in Divine Decree

The Muslim believes in the Qadha' and Qadar of Allah the Almighty. He believes in His Wisdom and Will, and that nothing in existence occurs or takes place except after Allah's Knowledge and allocation for it, and that He is just in his Decree and Will, Wise in His disposal and arrangement of affairs and that His Wisdom complies with His will. He is also convinced

---

[26] Ibid, 76

that whatever He does not will to happen will never occur and that there is neither power nor might except from Allah.[27]

The will of Allah is divine decree. It is this Will that controls the outcome of all actions in the universe. It is the measure of law regarding growth and development. It is commonly referred to as the Universal Law of Allah which is working throughout the entire creation of the universe. Within these boundaries, man is given free will.

It is paramount that the Muslim believes in the existence of faith; some may not believe its existence because of the inability to directly perceive. Islam argues that the inability to perceive something in no way is a direct implication that it does not exist. There are many natural phenomena in our universe that cannot be directly perceived. Most of the things that exist in our universe cannot be perceived by human logic, and this belief makes it reasonably possible to believe in the existence of a higher being. Faith in Islam means to submit to Allah not despite lack of evidence, but rather because proof of His Oneness of Lordship (Ar-Rububiyah) is overwhelming.[28]

It is the belief that true faith will manifest in the heart as sincerity in spoken words as affirmations and in the body as actions which are referred to as righteous deeds. Good deed is a direct result of sincere faith.

According to Islamic faith, it is not the acts alone that will get you into paradise or heaven (Jannah). It is only by the mercy of Allah that allows His people to enter paradise, *because there are not enough deeds that one person can do to deserve them to be entered into eternal paradise.*

In Islam, it is integral quality of faith to treat people in the manner you wish to be treated. Believers who have strong faith will perform many

---

[27] Ibid, 92

[28] abuaminaelias.com

righteous deeds, and those who have hearts tainted by spiritual disease have weak faith and perform not very many deeds of righteousness. These laws were created to help in understanding the choices one makes, as well as how choices affect life and soul evolution. These laws or ethics were set in place to govern human behavior. It is the order of the universe to influence moral behavior. They were greatly developed in the age of enlightenment, combining inspiration with philosophy, and later became the basis for social contact within humanity. They are natural contracts of natural law that use reason to analyze human nature. Historically, natural law has been about the use of reason to analyze human nature by acquiring a deeper understanding of the rules of moral behavior, via (dominant or insurgent) accounts of observed and/or posited aspects of reality and of "the human condition."

Self-Check

What do you believe about faith versus what someone told you to believe?

_____

_____

_____

_____

_____

_____

How can you express more gratitude in life?

_____

_____

_____

_____

_____

_____

4 unKonditional
UNIVERSAL PRINCIPLES

Whatever vibrational frequencies one projects out into the universe,
good, bad, or stoic, karmically returns to her without prejudice ...
Abundance is her birthright ... Fear is the prerequisite to lack ... yet,
fear is essential and ever present. Respecting fear, positive vibes, and
her belief is the kryptonite of fear, the key to abundance.

You've been exposed to my story, and by now you should know that I believe in a supreme being. I've given you plenty of reason to believe that your focus in the power of now absolutely must be supported by the annals of history and the fruits of the horizon. I've hopefully convinced you that you're not as smart as your IQ, but rather your emotions. I could talk about many religions, but I chose to highlight three monotheistic views of worship because of personal belief and my respect for the belief of others. I didn't select a pantheistic or polytheistic approach for the same reason, but I respect that others have their own beliefs and that none of us knows everything. Vibrational frequencies will penetrate the entire book because in everything we are and do, frequencies high or low are irradiated to, through, and from us and are critical to our "asmos" or continual growth in God and thus our life journey toward our Highest Good. In this Universe or Cosmos, all things are light years from chaos and were it not so, "not so" would we be. Regardless of your belief, I choose a belief that the complexity and view of the Universe or Cosmos could not be haphazardly constructed, and it took Wisdom, Intelligence, and Information to craft precision that allows life creation, evolution, and sustainment thereof.

The term Cosmos was introduced to us by the same guy who gave us $A^2 + B^2 = C^2$, applicable to right triangles where A and B sides are perpendicular to each other (90° angle), and the C represents the Cosmos! No not really, C is the hypotenuse, the incline or the longest side. Knowing either of two sides gives us the ability to derive the length of the third side from this equation or formula known as the Pythagorean Theorem. Pythagoras was a Greek philosopher, mathematician, scholar, and theologist who studied the universe just as Galileo and Aristotle, leaving us with insight that would vibrate through the ages like the frequencies we must be so mindful of. Many greats have expressed their love of humanity through astounding studies and contributions to aid the current and next generations to flourish, morphing into their greatest self or Highest Good, and they have given selflessly for the Greater Good and the repository of truth and preservation. That's what this chapter is about. While I cover some of these principles or Universal Laws in other sections of this work, I felt it prudent to dedicate a chapter to a few of the principles that I feel can steer us in the direction of deeper research, extra-unKonditional. For instance, I do not directly cover Hinduism. I do not give Buddhism it's stage time, nor do I elaborate on the similarities of Tao and Kabbalistic traditions, nor the Tree of Life most prominently devised by Rabbi Issac Luria in sixteen-century Palestine. I still respect them as they point to the Divine and spiritual righteous paths. So, I offer these Universal Laws to guide you on becoming a better, more productive and abundantly attractive you on your journey to your personal Highest Good.

i. The Law of Karma

Karma is defined as the sum of emotions in this and previous states of existence, viewed as deciding their fate in future existence. It is a derivation of the Sanskrit root "kri" and it means action. It is related to the Universal or Hermetic principle of Cause and Effect, just as the Law of Physics states, "for every action there is an equal and opposite reaction." So, for me, a person's reaction is in response to some type of causation. The reaction of the individual may be triggered, let's say, by a person's action witnessed by the individual whether directed at him or otherwise. For instance, an individual is in the close vicinity of an attempted assault and robbery of an elderly woman and he quickly intervenes by preemptive force. The intent, action and direction or vector of the action one makes will influence the reaction of the target and or witness and the returned resulting action for the initiator. Good karma is the result of good deeds as well as intent, and bad karma reflects bad intention and action. Whatever intention fuels an action, creates the karma that one experiences. One can mitigate suffering by learning lessons needed that will influence elevated intention. Behaving in righteous ways is the result of relying on the wisdom that resides within. It is that same wisdom that teaches one the lessons of life. Unfortunately for some, that is not always a reality. Some tend to learn best through pain. Since pain is necessary for growth, one karmically invites the experience of consequences in life. One does not understand the harm they have inflicted on others until it is inflicted upon them. When one is aware enough to make that connection, they can then modify their behavior to be sensitive and honorable in the actions they choose to enact concerning others.

It could also be an indication that whatever a person does to other people is what they do to themselves. Wisdom dictates that we make a conscious effort to do what's right for the Highest Good of all involved. Knowing and understanding best course of action requires that one listens to what the heart speaks. When one is cognizant of the law of karma it will certainly influence the idea that when good deeds and actions are committed, the universe responds with good deeds and actions. When one leads their life from a higher degree of love, then everything comes back to them in degrees of love. A person's actions are based upon their own conditioned free will, thereby creating certain consequences for their chosen action. Karma is just another way to term consequences or resulting effect.

Whatever vibrational frequencies one projects out into the universe, good, bad, or stoic, karmically returns to her without prejudice, for karma is produced through action and intention and knows no prejudice. Everything a person thinks, speaks, or does has karmic consequences.

ii. The Law of Duality

Duality is defined as being two-fold in nature, the state of being divided in two. One entity consisting of two extremes. It is more so concerned with Tao, that which produces and composes the universe. Tao is balance, the yin and yang. You can imagine yang as the centrifugal force causing an object moving in a curved path to veer away from the center of rotation. But centrifugal force requires the yin which is imagined as a centripetal force with force vectors constantly pulling into a rotating center controlling the waywardness of centrifugal force. Tao. This principle of the yin and yang, from a metaphysical perspective, is used in every facet of life. Another way of stating this is that everything, bar none, is a complex aggregate of universal energy composed of infinitely varying proportions of yin and yang, and we as humans can consider the yin our skin and the yang, our inner body.

From a perspective of interconnectedness on a macro level of the balance of creation, the yin and yang controls galaxies, universes, and the solar system to maintain order, and thus all universal laws, by the way, including the Law of Attraction. Without it, life and objects as we know them would be in a state of chaos, nonexistent and forever lost in a black hole where not even light is visible, yet detectable. Of course, then, there would be no life to detect it in the event of chaos except the Creator.

With Wisdom (B'reshit), God created the heavens and the earth or so it could be translated. Gen [2] *"The earth was without form, and void, and darkness was on the face of the deep ..." He then commanded the light to show itself,*

[4]*"And God saw the light, that it was good, and God divided the light from the darkness." (NKJV)* It is thought that the greater the difference in the yin and yang of a thing, the greater the force of attraction between them and vice-versa, they repel. So the further you are from the center of extremes the more aggressively you must thrive to reach the happy medium whether you are operating in the good or the bad extreme.

When one can align and come into balance with these energies, they begin to have a sense of clarity and connection to spirit. One's personal power is found within their perfected ability to be in balance with self. Duality expresses that any one entity, be it a person, belief, thought or situation will have opposite sides. In example, there's positive and negative, electrons and protons, right and wrong, left and right, love and hate, hot and cold, violence and peace, order and chaos, light vs darkness, emotional and rational, hard and soft, existent and nonexistent, heads and tails of a coin, ad-infinitum. According to this law, there is a happy medium, and it is about finding that middle ground and operating in that. A person cannot know one aspect of a thing without acknowledging the other. It is applicable in everything. Every person has within them the ability to operate in any extreme.

One cannot truly know oneself without having experienced or have been made aware of both extremes, but It is what that person chooses to accentuate. So in achieving your Highest Good, you must first realise that there is such a thing in comparison to where you are before you can even consciously begin. Allow me to explain. You must first know the meaning of good, then the meaning of bad. You can't desire fried African Lobster Tails if you never knew it existed, and once you are introduced to it, your food palate will determine if it's delectable or not. Unless you've learned to swim, you will not know the pleasure of swimming in a cave in the British Virgin Islands even if you were in the cave. Or you cannot know God if you never study His Word and know what your current state is. And even knowing him, you cannot know Him fully until He reveals all of whom He is to you, and if that's in the afterlife, it is what is with "I AM WHO I AM".

In life there should be balance. It is up to the individual to decide which extreme they choose to operate in. The conflict arises when there is belief that one aspect of a thing is better or worse than the other. Right or wrong is a construct of the ego. In spirituality there are no labels, just lessons. There is something to be learned from every experience. Rather than labeling everything good or bad, a better perspective to adopt would be to understand how each experience can lead to the higher elevations of the soul. Seeing things from one perspective only keeps one confined to a conditioned mindset. In the moment one makes decisions to evolve, everything in its opposite will come upon that person, thus forcing them to find middle ground and continue their chosen journey to reach their destined harmonic existence.

If you get this, then you are well on your way to your Highest Good. Operate in the positive realm of extremes of everything you do.

iii. The Law of Justice

This law speaks to what is good and right in life. Justice will always prevail. There is no time limit on when it prevails, but time will surely confirm that it always takes place exactly at the time it was destined to. Extend no credence nor justify worry for the injustices that may happen in life so long as one stands true to what is right in the heart. The need to be right and prove others wrong is behavioral egoistic tendency. As elevated or evolved spiritual beings, we learn to release any concerns about right and wrong and learn to trust that divine energy of our supreme being will set things in order according to what is fair and just. By divine design, all things will unfold as they should. Let go and let God. Living a life of submission affirms a belief that God is in control and things may not unfold the way our finite minds perceive. The attention is always toward things that feel right and correct in one's own life. Focused thought on light and love will increase fairness and justice in all things. Waste not time on situational comparison; the faithful belief in all things being in divine order should eliminate the desire to compare one's life or possessions to those of others. The concern should be to live true to one's own truth, and commitment to learn the lessons of the soul will create space for love and light to flow inward.

iv. The Law of Abundance

Abundance is her birthright. It is not just about financial gain. It rests upon the principle that there is an unlimited source of everything a person requires to live. God is the source of abundance. This law states that there is no lack anywhere, anytime. The belief in lack breeds lack of, keeping individuals out of alignment with abundance. This is much the same as ensuring that your heart and head is plumb. If one remains loyal to their belief that there is never enough, then there surely will never be enough. We have been conditioned to believe that lack is a way of life but lack is not a condition of the creator.

By design, the universe is abundant in all things. Everything in the universe is conscious. Because everything is conscious, a person's experience of lack or abundance is governed by the thoughts of that individual. Recall that we emanate vibes to the universe, and vibes which we send out return to us in the same manner, so it makes sense to vibrate out positive, high frequencies for greater returns of abundance as well. Limited thinking only limits the universe's ability to manifest abundance. The universe will only manifest according to the level of subconscious belief. Believe in abundance and the universe will manifest that reality. The key to abundance is gratitude. Don't just breeze through that point and move on. Meditate on it. Gratitude, being grateful for what one has today opens up space to receive more tomorrow.

Until one learns to become grateful in what they already have, they will not see how much more they can attain. When one is focused on gratitude for what they have, that produces and emits a different energy into the atmosphere, causing manifestation of something more than lack. As enlightened spiritual beings, it is our duty to hold, be, and express the light of the divine. After all, it was His wisdom that separated the light from the clutches of darkness, and why not then express His all knowing and loving light. Fear is the prerequisite to lack, and it hinders the manifestation of any abundance from the universe. However do not mistake this as encouragement to eliminate fear altogether.

According to Universal Law, everything is balanced and because of that belief, fear will always be relevant. It is not a promotion of the action of ridding fear from life, rather instruction to learn the trick of how to actuate within fear. Operating just beyond the realm of reality will help without hindering. One must give fear the permission to exist, and let it guide the way on this life journey. We must learn to work in harmony with fear. Any kind of discord that an individual holds within will negatively impact the free flow of abundance into one's life. Allow the fear to exist without allowing it to dominate and paralyze the essence of who you desire to become. As living expressions of the light of the divine, there should be specific awareness to one's own vibrating energetic field. Gratitude is surely an effective way to align oneself with abundance. Gratitude moves the focus away from lack. The universal law that governs life states that abundance already belongs to every living being. The grace of the infinite affirms it. The degree to which abundance is experienced depends greatly on how individuals have aligned themselves. We draw to us what is in alignment with our own energy.

v. Law of Divine Order

Everything is as it should be. This would be where trusting in the Infinite is a necessity. The path of least resistance leads one to a balanced and harmonious state. Being present in the moment is accepting divine order. Love and acceptance are natural parts of divine order. Everything happens as it is designed in its own time. It takes courage to release and trust that everything happens in divine order. Divine order is the essence of the creator. It is a belief that life unfolds in a manner that has already predestined our path. Whatever your belief on predestination given that there are varying views, Divine Order will influence your stance. As explained earlier in Garry Friesen's alternative view of God's will for your life, the Dot principle is not apparent and so remains a debated topic. Divine order is the intention of our higher self or soul to put us in situations that will teach the lesson needed for soul elevation. These are the lessons that teach us to attain the higher good of self and others. Connection to the divine requires stillness and centering. The soul requires this in order to communicate to the physical self the will of the divine. When one becomes centered, they are better able to connect to source. Divine order is the flow of spirit into the direction of life. Divine order is a sequence of events in the Cosmos according to the intention of the individual. It is what is set to happen based on the free will of one's decision. This means that whatever energy one projects, divine order says that same energy will return unto them.

vi. The Law of Soul Evolution

The human experience is designed to help the spiritual being evolve into the highest form of themselves, Highest Good. The path to enlightenment lessens the authority that fear has overtaken life. Elevated beings are not hindered by the threat of fear. Fear, unfortunately, is a part of reality, and one evolves when they learn to maintain mobility when it arises. Too often, we allow fear to paralyze us dead in our tracks, but the enlightened one acquires the tenacity to push through when fear pops up with his "scary ass." Soul evolution takes every mistake or perceived failure and uses it as an opportunity for growth. For it is the mistakes that are made that allows an individual the space to atone and evolve into a more harmonious being. Unconditional love is the focus of soul evolution. This law is responsive to the soul's desire to rise above fear-based emotion to live harmoniously in love and in peace. Being harmonious is evolutionary in the eyes of the soul. Serenity is what the soul craves. Self-mastery is the focal point in this classroom we call life. Self-mastery, in short, is maintaining self-control in any situation. Achieving this means one must be totally aware of all dimensions and accepting of one's own personality. One must be aware of all dimensions of their own personality to remain steadfastly in control. Knowing and understanding how not to be reactive to everything around us is the key component to mastering this level of control. It means having the ability to detach from volatile emotions and controlling instantaneous reaction. It is simply having control over one's own life.

Lack of control over one's emotions opens the door to vulnerability and exposure to the wiles of the wicked. The wicked get a rush from knowing that they can move you at will. Self-mastery thwarts such power in that the potential victim is able to rise above knee-jerk reactions by keeping a cool head. The adage "he who angers you controls you" is true. Being in-tune with self is mastery to reject intentional manipulation of others. Even in times of transformation, there are some who only want to prove that no change has taken place. It takes patience and grace with self to reach that level of control. Discontinue allowing oneself to be infected with the negative energy of wayward beings whose goal is to get other people riled up. Security in oneself is vital and brings about stability. The aligning of one's mind, body, and spirit is conducive to stability in a peaceful existence as well as experience.

vii. The Law of Gratitude

Gratitude is about contentment. It is the appreciation of anything already in one's possession. It is the backbone of peace. Ridding oneself of anxiety because of the things they do not have or cannot control only begets more anxiety and blocks flow of what is meant to come. Being gracious is about making the best of whatever one has without feeling anxious because of what one thinks they need. Change in perspective makes gratitude necessary. Complaining is only the result of perception. Abundance results from gratitude, and lack results from complaining. The more grateful one is for all that they have, the cosmos will provide more of the same. When genuine gratitude is shown, the cosmos reads peace, love, and thankfulness in that individual's energy field. The universe, being created from pure energy of love will facilitate the same experience that influences the feelings and emotions of love and peace. Having the ability to receive those things the universe intends for one to experience suggests one is in a constant state of gratitude. Gratitude unlocks the fullness of life as it turns that which we have into enough.

Our thoughts emit energetic frequencies, and having an abundant mentality will eliminate the existence of lack in one's mind. Diminishing limiting beliefs in one's mind opens space for the things that are desired to manifest. Expressing gratitude is empowering in the sense that people no longer question whether they can or will receive the things they desire. We express gratitude through deeds and thoughts. We give it without the intent to receive. We should express it for all blessings. Gratitude weakens negativity in one's life. It is quite difficult to complain about anything when the focus is on things that bring peace and harmony. It is an outward expression of love and sense of appreciation.

When the focus is on appreciation, it becomes easy to bless others. The way to increase feelings of gratitude in one's life would be to mentally make note of the things that one is grateful for in life. Gratitude brings peace for today and creates a vision for tomorrow.

Self-Check

What do you see in these Laws that reveal you as your own worst enemy?

_____

_____

_____

_____

_____

_____

_____

How can you benefit immediately from these Laws?

_____

_____

_____

_____

_____

_____

_____

5 unKonditional LOVE

Agapos Agape

Agapos is the Greek word attributed to God connoting that God is Love. In turn, God's unconditional and supernatural love for us is Agape. 1John states it well.

1 John 4:7 "Let us love one another, for love is of God; and everyone who loves is born of God and knows God. He who does not love does not know God, for God is love." (KJV)

Love is more than just, "I love you." Love is a complex set of emotions, behaviors, and beliefs associated with strong and/or intense feelings of affection, protectiveness, warmth, or fondness for another person. True testaments of love are outward expressions of the emotions felt in one's heart for other people. It is a genuine outgoing concern for others. The Greek, including Aristotle, studied, named, classified and characterized love. They ascribed eight names to forms of love, six of which I incorporate, applying to my experiences, and the other two are honorable mentions.

- Agape - God's unconditional love, Classified as Familial

- Storge (Stor-gi or Stor-gay)- Familial, also Classified as Friendship

- Eros - Romantic, Classified as Romantic

- Philia - Friendly, Platonic, Classified as Friendship

- Philautia - Self-love, Classified as Friendship

- Pragma - Practical, Classified as Romantic

- Mania - Obsessive and Possessive, Classified as Romantic narrowly

- Ludus - Playful, Classified as Romantic

The essence of unconditional love, agape, is for one to embody the capacity to love another person past their pain, past their faults without expectation. Agape is not only about loving other people past their pain but also about allowing oneself to love past their own pain. Too often, it is our pain that prohibits us from loving others unconditionally or conditionally.

Even more obstinate than a black hole, our walls of protection are covered in the poison ivy of pain and gripped by the vines of disappointment, restricting the flow of love from either penetrability or escape.

I mean, at least a black hole allows matter to enter in, but our pain shuts all traffic down in both directions! Because Agapos is unconditional in all that He is, we should strive to love just as He does. Love is a natural affection for people and is intrinsic in all beings. Agapic love is supernatural, and it meets people wherever they are. Each person is to grow into whoever they decide to be. It is the duty of everyone to show love by allowing grace for others in troublesome times. The willingness to love another person past limiting circumstance is what unconditional love looks like. Love does not make commitments alone. While love is complex, like any other emotion, it can sometimes be fickle. We base commitment on love and decision. When decisions are made to love someone unconditionally in good or stoic circumstances, the commitment to each other is rarely in jeopardy.

Agape is the preeminent love, for it is the pinnacle of love offering with spirit as it's catalyst. It is unparalleled in that it desires nothing in return and will accept whatever karma comes back to it, even if that is zero. Without expectation, one chooses to bless one with agapic love no matter the circumstance, even intentional demolition type influences or activities. In the construct of Agape, there is no physical attraction or intimate act, rather it's a feeling. It is thought, though, that acts of Philautia can elicit Agape since self-governance, due to self-love, produces results.

It is the Spirit which excites Agape within an individual, and agapic love can only operate within the realm of the Highest Good of the individual. My sister operated in this realm when she and her husband chose me after the death of our mother who instilled in us this spirit of love, but she showered me with a combination of Storge and Agape. I realize that she is my sister, but I must say that she and her husband took love to new heights, and, for that selfless embrace, I am eternally grateful.

Her spirit spawned purpose beyond her being big sis', and I am convinced that it was her spirit, tutored by the spirit of mamma, that made it seamless to pick up the responsibility of drawing me into her and showering me with such amazing, supernatural love, nurturing and care. Her husband dispensed grace effortlessly in supporting her decision and granting me a sense of stability and family past our loss. It is my hope and in my optimistic, maybe naive, estimation that if we offered the supernatural naturally, through feelings, we might moderately impact the world which would be driven to act in the realm of our Highest good for the Greater Good of humanity. I just know that in perpetuity, it has a grandiose effect on how I navigate life.

It is trivial to base love in relationships on emotion alone, though there's nothing trivial about but rather to Agapic love. This is such a profound statement, and I pray that you get it, really get it. If you struggle with it, that's ok, I'll explain. Feelings are an integral part of one's life to serve as indicators on how one relates to self and other people, and the nature of Agapic love being a feeling rather than an act seats it on the throne of all love. It is Love of all love. But it should not be a foundation in any relationship. Stay with me. Because emotions are fickle, we allow them to guide us in deciding to unconditionally love those individuals we commune with daily. When a person has feelings about the well-being of another person, they commit to uphold that relationship on a solid and lasting foundation. Feelings change and so do people. No individual is perfect, and there is a level of dysfunction in all of us. The decision to be in a relationship with someone is also about making a choice to accept the other person's level of dysfunction or imperfection. We have a choice to accept or reject certain things in the realm of relationships. Some levels of dysfunction may be more difficult to accept, so it is all about what one will tolerate. So, here is the crux of the matter. Agape, as described, cares not and finds all the dysfunction trivial, and so isn't expecting anything in return. It loves through hardship, heartache, heartbreak, inconceivable circumstances, and all sorts of dysfunction. It can be said plainly in this way, "All things are trivial to Agape, however, there is nothing trivial about Agape." Its characteristics embody the classification of Familial love, not Romantic love. Eros, Ludus, Pragma, and Mania fall into the classification of romance.

Key components of a solid foundation in relationships are a good mix of decision, honesty, respect, communication, and trust. Agape isn't concerned with any of that; it's on the level of grace and mercy. It is by God's grace that we should be so fortunate as to be caught up in the rapture of love and take up residency with Him in Paradise.

i. The Law of Unconditional Love

I dare to say that, as our Creator, we have a natural affinity for God innately implanted deep within our soul. The same is true of the vessel who "birthed and nurtured" us from day one. [Traditional Surrogates, gestational surrogacy, egg donation, abandonment, and adoption of any sort not considered here, though the studies may completely surprise you! Go to https://www.ncbi.nlm.nih.gov/pmc/articles/PMC3210890/ if interested] Naturally, we fight for survival, communicating our needs from birth, though we can't speak. But our centeredness depends on something far more powerful than any other characteristic classifying us, and that thing drives our behavior, given it's strength or weakness—love of self.

A healthy love of self first is the most important trait a person can possess. This does not rub against the Law of Liberty introduced in Deuteronomy, rather it enforces it. Loving oneself first does not equate to selfishness, it equates wholeness, honor and survivability. When a person loves themselves unconditionally, they become free to love others the same. Unconditionally loving self indicates honoring one's truest heart's desire. This law makes it possible that the love of self will attract the same love from others. The law of unconditional love honors that which serves the Highest Good of self and others. Honoring the truest desires of the heart is how one honors God. Because God lives within, honoring the Highest Good of self and others honors God intrinsically. We owe no one full disclosure of our personal life, but we owe it to ourselves to be authentic in the truth we tell ourselves. Whatever serves in our own Highest Good is what will serve the Greater Good, the Highest Good of all. Unconditional love is the total acceptance of others for who they are without expectation, judgment, or a desire to change them. There is no sense in manipulating others by anything other than the shining example of your own loving behavior.

Unconditional love, agape, prevails in spite of flaws. The law of unconditional love causes one to believe that there is love in everyone. Law commands us to love, even in difficult moments when the light in others emits tenuously. We base the behavior of most people on the conditioning of their surroundings and other people's opinion. Even in destructive behavior, love should still exist within. It is vital to understand that most people behave according to their experiences of childhood and early adulthood. Though experiences may be different, it does not give one permission to dismiss and treat others as if they are the lesser, inferior or worse, counterfeit. Because someone is not behaving according to established standards does not make it acceptable to degrade their character. That's the time to be open, to understand from a place of non-judgment, individualism and absence of expectation. No matter the behavior, all people deserve love. No one is licensed to judge another simply because the display of behavior is foreign to their own. It is the duty of the enlightened individual to love without condition, offering grace to those who may not have grown to a higher level of being. And even more astute, one who claims enlightenment must recognize and respect cultural differences which appear within the wide spectrum of acceptable behavior.

Unconditional love knows no bounds. That classifies it limitless. When one loves without limit, the love they are entitled to is of the same class. Living in a state of grace gives way for love to flow without dictating how it flows. Unconditional love extends forgiveness the chance to remain open for resolution to manifest. The person who loves unconditionally understands that other people may not love or behave in a mirrored fashion. That is why it is crucial to understand how other people express love. Realise that unique experiences cause others to see, live, and love differently. One must remain open to understanding that love may not be reciprocated in the way one might expect. Because love may not come in the way one has conditioned themselves to believe does not imply that love does not exist. Unconditional love understands others may not have the capacity to love. The degree to which a person receives love should not determine how love is rendered. However, we must be careful not to confuse differences in expressions of love with subtle emotional abuse.

Others may very well express love in different ways, but not to the point that it becomes tedious and hurtful. Love should never feel like abuse or cause undue harm to the heart. Negative energy disrupts the flow of love and taint the way love is expressed. Ulterior motive characterized as selfish gain can taint our expression of love. Genuine love does not inflict harm intentionally. I think it best to understand the practice of giving and receiving love to avoid any attempt to manipulate one's expression of love.

Positive reinforcement of those activities which bring joy increases the chances of having memorable experiences manifest in one's relationship. Reinforcing unfavorable attributes in others will sadly introduce tension into the relationship, driving a wedge between the parties, causing a core meltdown. No one wants to be constantly reminded of their flaws; its nothing less than insensitive. So, it's counterproductive to needle one with disparaging remarks and criticism of their character and/or features. Realise first that you are imperfect, and, therefore, calling out the imperfections of others is a bit narcissistic. The divine grace of God can heal and change the creation far better than we can. The love that one has within will govern the outward display of love to others. Love is universal and expressed in various forms. The possibility of unconditional love is endless and always available. The catch is to persuade others of it.

Seemingly all too often, we meet the search for unconditional love with a bag of conditions. Love filtered through conditional pretenses suffers limitation. Often times people can become so engrossed in finding unconditional love for themselves that they lose sight of unconditionally loving others. All one would need to do in loving themselves without limit is to practice patience and grace with self, then extend that same patience and grace to others. Everything in life starts with self, so we must show kindness to ourselves first. Whatever is on the inside will reveal itself in time. One thing's for certain, people cannot deviate from what is natural for too long. A person's behavior is a telltale sign of what lives within their very essence. Love is universal, and the message is the same in any culture, which is a message of kindness and concern. Love encompasses a range of positive emotion that ranges from deep personal affection to simple pleasure. Reasoning would argue that we were simply designed that way, as human beings have tendencies to express love on a robust gradient of intensity. The polarity of love illuminates a continuum of positive and negative attributes. Love can be considered positive and negative with its virtue representing human kindness, compassion, and affection, as "the unselfish loyal and benevolent concern for the good of another": its vice representing human moral flaw akin to vanity, selfishness, amour propre [upper range of self-esteem], and egotism, as it leads people into a mania of obsessiveness and codependency.[29]

ii. Philautia

Love of self, philautia, is the variant of love classified as the healthy love one has for oneself. It is excited by the soul which realizes one's own emotional, physical and psychological needs which enhances your spirit. Before anyone can effectively dispense love, they must first be filled with love of self. Self-love is not only about taking care of one's physical needs, it is also about satisfying one's mental, emotional, and spiritual well-being. The benefits of loving oneself first are astronomical. Cutting the chatter of the crowd can be scary. It takes time and trust to develop a fearless devotion to the voice of the soul. On my path to total self-acceptance, I had to learn and understand the many parts of my personality. By living that truth, I discontinued trying to find and fix the things that other people said needed changing, and I focused on the things I felt needed attention. As I continued to stare at that faded reflection in the mirror, I realised that I had given far too much of myself away to get next to nothing in return. The more I made myself available, the more depleted I felt.

It was time I started feeding my own soul. I could no longer give so much of myself that my reserves were bone dry, and my heart was emotionally empty, flatline broke. On the cusp of emotional bankruptcy,

---

[29] Roget's Thesaurus (1998) p. 592 and p. 639

either I would need to file for Chapter 11 to stave off so-called lien-holders (more like lien-poachers), send out an S.O.S. signal for emotional rescue of the heart, or perform emergency self CPR. "Love me!" screeched my heart, and no one was listening, not even me. I realised at some point that I had heard it, but faintly. I say faintly because I wasn't listening in the truest sense of the word, and love of self had to originate within me. For self-preservation, I had to learn to set boundaries, refusing to lay my heart on the line for anyone not willing to act from a place other than their own selfish greed. Loving myself enough to let go, I jettisoned those leeches who bled my heart dry. Reciprocity was important to me, and I had to love me enough to preserve my love for those who would return love. The desire to find and fix the change in others became less necessary. It was clear to me that it wasn't my place to fix anyone; that is the work of our divine creator, God.

The desire to change other people, in theory, makes that person a worker of witchcraft, and I have no desire to change anyone for my own personal benefit. I give people the benefit of the doubt and space to be who they believe themselves to be. I have learned to govern myself accordingly. The choice to engage or not is mine and mine alone. Making a choice to disengage does not mean that I am choosing to hold a grudge of any sort. Holding a grudge is holding on to anger. Holding on to anger is detrimental to who I am and what I believe in. No longer will I hold on to ill feelings, because I gave myself permission to feel my genuine feelings, and it has become easier to release them after I have taken the time to understand them and why they exist. I understand that what I do to self is what I do to other people. That said, I don't want to hold on to negative energy within myself, so I must not hold on to negative energy regarding others.

No longer focusing on the changes others thought I needed to make, I became better able to just be and relax on a low resistance current to my Highest Good. My focus tilted inward, I studied my own behavior and figured out attributes and ways I needed to adjust and tweak that would allow for me to become the person I desired to be. And in doing so, I postured myself to be in life's flow of least resistance. I am learning to allow the change to occur by the hand of the Infinite working on my behalf. I also realise that change and evolution is a lifelong process (-asmos), so I learned to let go of the ego's need to change everything in an instant. That dependency on the Infinite protects the integrity of genuine love which is too precious to have ever been taken for granted. That lesson taught me to be okay with whatever other people thought about me and with my decision to bow out gracefully and peacefully on each occurrence. It used to bother me a great deal to think anger spiked in someone, me being the target and catalyst for whatever reason. I soon learned to let them think whatever they chose.

Truth is, if they were not willing to hear my heart, then it didn't matter what I said. They were going to believe what they wanted to believe either way, and I became at peace with that. I just couldn't keep sacrificing myself for people who would not make the same sacrifices for me. And why should you? If your situation is similar, you should walk — no no no — run! Run in the complete opposite direction.

This taught me the valuable lesson of self-love. One inevitable truth in life is that people are their own worst critics. I was harder on myself than I was on anyone else. Yep, I hear it all the time; it's what we do to ourselves. It was hard learning to show kindness to me, because I was perfectly comfortable beating up on myself. Sound familiar? Loving self first and being true to what mattered most to me became my priority.

Unconditional love of self is not absent love for others but a conscious effort to have love for self. One cannot pour from an empty cup, nor dispense from an empty dispenser, so being filled with honor, concern, and love of self is essential to loving others and most importantly to living a healthy and balanced life of peace and serenity. It's not far to serenity, for this never never land lives within you. Ask Christopher Cross, I'm sure he would agree. :-)

Unconditional love says, "I will allow myself the chance to love again after heartbreak." You should pray on this and speak it out loud, for it will surely take some convincing. But listen, you owe it to your loving, emotional, fragile, humane self. Only God knows the depth of heartbreak we have experienced, and despite our fears, we must trust God in that His promise is true in that He will not fail His children.

Unconditional love of self means love is available even in dark moments of uncertainty. All we need to do is learn to tap into that circuit, that junction box which empowers us to love through the reddish muck and mire of our "Georgia clay of pain."

Maybe this is not your experience — but maybe so — In a lot of ways, I felt like God betrayed me, and that was a hard truth to cough up, and I hadn't a clue as to how to apply the Heimlich maneuver to get it from deep within and past the tip of my tongue. Fearful, I finally took a risk, found the strength and — come what may — I admitted this to God. Oh boy — what a pregnant pause.

I waited.

And waited.

And waited.

And braced myself.

And cried out of fear.

And waited some more.

Virtual silence — you could hear a colony of ants marching, every exterior sound amplified.

Subconsciously, I counted in my head to I don't know what — probably 1000's upon 1000's.

I watched the clock on my wrist, on my cell phone, on the wall and nothing happened. The phone didn't so much as chime.

Still concerned and skeptical, I walked lightly on pins and needles.

The lights were still on, the roof didn't cave in, the sky wasn't falling and I wasn't Chicken Little — but I could have been.

The brave yet submissive soul in me speaks to you with great joy. I survived that verbal admission to God, but I think that had everything to do with my total submission to Him. And even in my fear, I trusted that he would forgive and heal me for the feeling that I had carried for so long. Maybe we all need to come clean with God, verbally, because He already knows our hearts. I believe He wants us to be candid with Him, and that opens the door for us to receive Him in all His power and glory. The Divine grace of God can make changes and heal exceptionally, far better than we can.

All I needed to do was love myself without limit and practice patience and grace with myself first. I have become better able to not punish myself for my own thoughts or mistakes. It is abusive when you don't handle self-first with the love and care you wish from others. That was something I was not very good at and still sometimes struggle with. So, don't sweat the struggle, just keep plowing the field of Higher Good; Maybe, we'll get there together. I would beat myself up when I faltered. I realise now that mistakes meant I was human and that my missteps didn't define my integrity or character.

Everything in life starts with self. We can only be or grow into best self when first we learn to love the upside down "We" — "Me" unconditionally. I choose not to place any restraint on what is necessary for me to live and be at my Highest Good at full capacity. And that's just it, it's your choice! This world deserves the very best of who we are, authentically, at our core.

I cannot and would cheat the world by presenting it with a watered-down version of who I am and who God created me to be. You should say this in prayer. And say it out loud repeatedly. Say it until it's ingrained within your soul, your daily walk, and every action from wake up to reading the backs of your eyelids at night, or at the end of your shift or modified day. Operating in ways that dishonor the authenticity of who we are is just that, dishonest. And dishonesty has a tendency to come with a hefty price tag. I will not downplay my true heart because the truth of who we are takes up residency in that amazingly unique space.

You have a bright future of grand potential. That future takes planning and action. So plan to understand the entire center of your being, then repeat after me:

Once I learn and understand the entire center of my being, I can pour from a heart that overflows with the purest most gentle love I can muster. I operate in and of my highest self when I govern myself according to what lives within my soul, escaping judgment. Only then can others see the best in me exclusively because I present myself in the fullness of the light of the divine. I declare this — that perfectly imperfect nurtured kernel which lives within will manifest. When it breathes, grows, and connects on the vine of the divine, others will be compelled to reciprocate.

Establishing boundaries is an excellent way to guard one's emotional well-being. One's boundaries protect personal principles and maintain specific standards of behavior by stipulating what is and is not acceptable, guiding others to behave honorably in the space of he who's boundaries are defined. Self-love is about owning one's total truth and unapologetically living out loud according to what one believes to be true for that individual's own life. Setting clear boundaries is key to ensuring that relationships remain respectful. They set the limit for acceptable behavior of individuals one may interact with, minimizing opportunity for misunderstanding, offensively laced assumptions and the probability of being taken for granted or taken advantage of. You'll know when you need to enforce, set, or establish a new set of boundaries to put unwanted behavior in check.

Weak boundaries will leave a person vulnerable for becoming the victim of offenses of undesirable conduct from others. Having clear boundaries will teach others how to treat us. They also will protect a person from exploitative relationships and help to avoid getting too close to people who have mal intent. Prudence would encourage removal of oneself from relationships that no longer serve a meaningful purpose in your life. We can all agree to the pointless nature of holding on when there is nothing left to hold on to. Loving others from across the street does not negate the action or existence of love; it just means that others have made a choice not to behave according to the boundaries set. When people fail to love you enough to honor your space, time, wishes, and principles, then they violate you as a human being and, so, have not earned even the thinnest measure of your energy, time, or attention.

Having willingly disrespected you, especially without remorse, they must take a back seat and lose access to you. When one loves unconditionally, the selfless act of respecting boundaries of others is second nature, proving they care enough not to chance the loss of someone they want to experience life with. So, they effortlessly honor whatever's necessary as an ambassador of peace and a catalyst for greater trust and intimacy within the relationship.

Living out loud refers to living with confidence in what one believes to be true. It gives a person no permission to mistreat others and address them in condescending ways. There is a certain level of humility in living out loud. It is a fearless calm that lives in the individual who lives with purpose and control. Unconditional love says, "I don't mock and put people down who may not have arrived in the same place as I." Love is about service. If we are to be of service to others, it is essential to first be of service to oneself. It is impossible to serve and love others from a state of fatigue. Honor, concern, and love of self are crucial for living a healthy and balanced life. Before love can go out, it has to live within. Cutting the chatter of other people's opinions and learning to live in soul consciousness heightens the experience of peace within oneself. It takes time and trust to develop a fearless devotion to the voice of the soul, but it is time well spent. Patient mindfulness connects soul to source. That connection allows the flow of communication into spirit from the Spirit of the creator.

It is my belief that personality has many dimensions. For me to know and accept myself, it meant it was time that I acknowledged every aspect of my own personality and gained clarity on the things I valued in life as opposed to what other people told me I should value. It meant I had to honor the things that were of value to that dimension of who I am. As I lived more in that truth, I discontinued the attempts to find and fix the things that other people said were wrong, and I focused on the things that mattered most to me. I soon figured out that most people only wanted to change those parts of me they could not control. As I continued to stare at the faded reflection in the mirror, I had given too much of myself away. It would not have been so bad had I been getting the same in return, but that just wasn't the case. That is why I appreciate having people who feed my soul and not people who solely feed off my soul. Therein lies the problem; it is not at all practicable to give more of oneself to those who are not willing to reciprocate.

Life and relationships are about give and take; I had done more than my share of giving, requiring nothing in return, exhausting my center of benevolence and transference. Give, give, give. And what would they do? Take, take, take! We've all probably experienced this type of relationship on some level, friendship or otherwise. The more I gave, the more vigorously some would take, never mirroring my generosity. For those of you who have experienced this, you know very well what I'm talking about. For me, this was the people pleasing dimension of my personality. This was the part of me that believed the more I gave to others, the more my chances of losing them would decrease. I really hope that very few of you are paddling that same kayak. It wasn't the revolving door of fleeting relations that frightened me though, it was the pain that ensued from losing someone that terrified me. Screeeeam! The pain of loss triggered something traumatic for me, and I wanted to avoid that at all costs.

So, I overextended myself to give everybody what they needed, hoping that they would in turn give me what I needed. I didn't even realise that was the bill of goods I had been selling myself for so long. The more I gave of me, the more others expected me to give. I don't know about you, but my vending machine couldn't withstand a constant tilt, rocking, and shakedown, dispensing emotional snacks without a viable ROI, neither Return nor "Restock" on Investment. So, I made an executive decision to dissolve the vend business of selling myself short. Accepting that some only loved me when they got all their wants fulfilled, left me feeling empty, tilted, and needful in the wrong sense, but I kept on allowing the glut out of fear of loss while I was emotionally famished. It was that decisive moment that I discontinued the service they expected that rubbed them the wrong way, inducing friction. Instantaneously, I became undesirable, and that was problematic. Because I was responsible for catering to people by spoiling them freely with everything they demanded without resistance or seeking an equal and opposite demand, I stepped up and owned my participation in creating that beast.

Changing that narrative allows me to now understand the importance of fending for self and reciprocity. It begs that I share with you that we cannot sacrifice self for relationships that refuse to reciprocate, yielding what we need to feed our desires. The time arose to recant, overextending myself for what I wanted and needed. So, yes, it was me who needed to straighten the tilt, lean back and stand up for self. It was I who changed. We must make that change for we, regardless of someone else's unfair demand. And if it means that you are forever referred to as undesirable for deciding to protect you, then you should laugh in the face of slander. I now am impervious to such wayward labels. Anything other than me standing up straight for what I require is problematic for me, regardless of anyone's characterization of my desirability. If my heart is misunderstood at this point, that's just the way it is, because I refuse to work overtime to prove that I am enticing and worthy in the estimation of another human suction cup ever again. Get rid of those suction cups before they suck the life out of you, and I mean that in the literal sense for many of you. We are beautiful people, whether woman or man, and we deserve love that truly loves us back with respectable Return on Investment (ROI).

The time arrived for me to feed my own soul. I no longer give unfettered access to me, meaning so much of myself that I am a faded reflection, unrecognizable and jaded with a permanently scarred heart. Becoming the object of someone's obsession turned venomous taught me, critically, that I must set boundaries to protect against emotional outrage stemming from the selfishness of others and my choice of noncompliance. And so, I attached safety fetters to my heart and soul, and it would take Prince Charming and his cast of servants bearing gifts of pure joy to waltz in with the keys and combinations to get past gatekeepers of the highest level of security to even be worthy of subsequent stages of a mutual relationship. Well, you know what I mean. I served others because it is in my heart to serve, but I had to learn to set boundaries. I can't begin to stress this enough; you must set boundaries according to your morals and comfort zone or you will be throwing your pearls to swine, and you will be trampled and devoured like slop. Jesus said it — I experienced it routinely. The realisation is that we need not just a casual but at least a reasonable and reciprocal ROI on love, and that means change must be initiated and implemented by us setting the parameters around how we want to be engaged, respected and fulfilled.

There was a stark realisation that because of my genuine concern, there were some situations I allowed myself to remain in, situations that would end in disaster. The failure hinged on their imperiling need for validation which outweighed the support I could offer versus what they required of me. Let's just say they were needy situations, and I was the unwilling participant, but because I stayed and was privy to the consequences, I again would be impervious to being discarded like dirty rags. I was fine because I knew in my heart that my intentions were pure and for that reason, I will not hold on to any ill feelings. There was no logical reasoning to fester up feelings of hurt or anger when I already expected to be the object of frustrated emotions, given preconditions. If ever the opportunity presented itself for those in want of validation or proof that they were worthy of the need they so desperately sought, targeting me was a given if I didn't honor the want. That kind of behavior is typical in those who lack the validation they need the most. When you know and understand the people you are dealing with, it becomes much easier to allow the chips to fall where they may. It doesn't cut as deep when that person double crosses you. Those situations taught me how to transcend the outer layer of a person and see things from their point of reference.

Doing that helped me to take my ego off the table. Now, that doesn't mean that I am even remotely saying that it's ok for you to be a doormat to be trampled in any situation, nor am I condoning my own behavioral choice to stick around fully aware of the peril of pearls to come. But what I do impress upon you is that sometimes we stick it out for whatever reason, and we must in that scenario chastise ourselves before getting upset with the situation or the individual for expected and a behavioral rendering with the colors of lashing out. Does that make sense? If we know the end result, and the end result is perilous for us or even the other party, and we have the ability to escape the situation and unwittingly choose not to, we must be ready to accept the consequences. It's a no brainer. We are just as much at fault as the perpetrators, and in that sense, where's the need for crying about it — point blank? Now, will I allow myself to become that same doormat as before or should you ever? That's a resounding No! We can only govern ourselves and guard against bad relationships and the non-preferable behavior of others when there is a communications or situational relationship break down.

And then there were others; I knew that evil dwelt within their spirit, and I turned the other cheek because I wanted to believe my love would be enough, but that proved to be a waste of time. I needed a relationship with those who would love me past their need for service. I wanted to surround myself with people who wanted nothing from me but me. It seemed at one point everybody wanted extraordinary from me, and I did whatever I could to provide until there was nothing left to give.

I speak the absolute rawest truth of what is on my mind, and my delivery was sometimes abrasive, but I have never been intentional in hate or disdain for anyone. While hate is a degree of love, I am not advocating hatred and we should never act on anything that does not serve the Highest Good of self and others. I have made mistakes and made poor choices, but my intentions have never been malicious. My intention was to figure out how I was showing up in relationships because not only did I desire to be a better person, I also wanted to be a better friend or lover or relative, relation dependent. I realised that in some areas I governed myself in a way that made others feel as if they could not confront me. Perhaps I took protecting myself too far. So we want to be careful of being a puffer fish, blowing self out of proportion to fend off aggression but seeming unapproachable to partners or any close relation. All my life I have been softhearted, and they teased me for it, so I felt I had to appear fierce and unapproachable to protect myself. I could only grow into my best self when I first learned to love me unconditionally. And loving myself unconditionally meant that I had to deflate the mask, lose the puffer-face, accept and acknowledge all my insecurities and love me anyway. In changing my mind, I made a covenant with myself to know, acknowledge and accept that I don't have to live my life from a state of heartbreak or behind an exaggerated mask.

We can be free to give love and let love in by opening up to new thought patterns and allowing the right people and relationships into our heart's grande foyer. Free yourself and no longer be strapped, bound and gagged by fears of abandonment. Just meditate on positivism, believe, and actuate with this in mind:

"The considerate who walk this journey beside me will endure, and I will not be forced to work 'til exhaustion attempting lasting connections. The weak at heart will vanish into the night, and I will release memory to run with and wish them well. But the pure at heart will summon the strength to glide through rough waters of the light and anchor down in the calmness of the night. My love will go out like an apostle, a messenger pigeon, and return with affirmation of mutual racing of the heart. And Veritable Love will love Love without boundary even as boundaries are mutually and aesthetically pleasing. When Love is too genuine to waste on the greatest of ingrates, turn away and never look back lest you become as salty as the love of Lot. While we are not perfect by any means, we are perfectly imperfect and deserving of love returned as it is sent. Putting our best effort forward is sufficient, and a pure heart will attract a quandary of curious variety, but only the veritable at heart shall enter the foyer of Untainted Love."[30]

Victor Trionfo 2021

---

[30] Trionfo, Victor (Alias), Editor in Chief, Veritable Quandary of Untainted Love

Self-Check

What conditions prohibit you from loving yourself and others unconditionally?

_____

_____

_____

_____

_____

_____

_____

What dimensions of your personality do you hide behind a mask?

_____

_____

_____

_____

_____

_____

_____

6 unKonditional FAMILY

*... my outer layer has experienced macro-evolution; I've transformed
into teflon coated kevlar, frictionless and strong...
Your daily life-sized Instagram may not always draw likes, but there
should always be authentic emoji hearts of love.*

Storge

"The variant of love that is associated with family." Storge, pronounced [Stor-gay or Stor-gi (gee)], is that offspring love which is born, lives, and breathes within a family unit. It is sacrificial and instinctual. It metaphorically incarnates and is invested with the familial body sworn to security, safety, support, and unconditional love for those it embodies. Storge love is a love of unity. Storge can sometimes be used to describe sexual relationships that were born out of friendship. In the sense that friends can sometimes become lovers. This degree of love falls under storge because it can be difficult to define the moment that friendship developed into love. There is a significant amount of emphasis placed on commitment among storgic lovers. But here, the main focus is on familial love.

Family takes on a very different meaning for different people and is defined on a continuum of varied meaning. The word family is rooted in the Latin word famulus. Famulus is defined as servant. I envisage families coming together for the purpose of being in service to each other. I believe that the soul reincarnates and that it does so because there is something it needs from a specific family dynamic to develop and be of higher service to self and others.

Family should be about togetherness, a coming together of individuals to experience oneness of body and spirit. Each individual member of the family is important because they serve their unique purpose. They should each be willing to pour back into the family unit that which they withdraw. It is a give and take on a broader scale. Like all relationships, family relationships are about the exchange of love, respect, and support. Unconditional love of family means to love despite mistakes, not withhold love because of them. There is a difference in genuine mistakes and intentional abuse of family. We should not compromise the integrity of the family because of disloyalty or unfaithfulness. It is more about the collective than it is about one individual.

The concept is wrapped with a bright yellow ribbon that insinuates that being related to one another makes you family. However, the real and unfortunate truth is this; Nothing can be farther from the truth. Family is about holding and sharing a sacred bond. We should not consider it an obligation to anyone. However, it should be about the desire to sacrifice anything that threatens to harm that bond. This special bond should make up the sanctity of what God intended of the family collective. A family bond should be one that binds souls together for a lifetime, but within the construct of the modern family, that is not even remotely close to being an option. Families are dysfunctional and filled with melodrama. Familial relationships reek of passive aggression. They are riddled with cliques and are devastated by immense separation. The family divide grows further and further apart with each passing year, resembling canyons of the Midwest. Because society has conditioned us to live sporting an "all about me" mindset, we have allowed division to be the solution at the slightest disagreement or misunderstanding. And to some extent, I can relate, respecting why the division takes place.

We must protect our own peace of mind, even with the misbehavior of family. Being related to people does not mean that people have a pass to mistreat a relative. True, there are just some situations or pain that a person cannot recover from as quickly as we might assume. I don't make excuses for these situations nor think it's right, but it is what it is, a true reality. I would be remiss to paint a perfect picture in rose-colored frames when the truth is consistent in most every family I have known. Families are filled with so many personalities that have a mix of good and sometimes unbecoming characteristics. And if one wants to protect their peace, they may deem it necessary to love at a distance, not an option admired, but a potential necessity in truth none-the-less.

Hurt and disappointment lie at the root of family distancing, and in today's day, COVID-19 is a co conspirator. Families have unlearned the art of standing together. Latter generations possibly never learned it because we have been divided within families for years. Forget the COVID, we are that virus. The new generation does not know the truth or mechanics of what caused the breakdown from the beginning. This is an unfortunate circumstance and truth within my family. Inevitably, you are touched by the same within your immediate family or circle of friends, associates, or acquaintances.

As for me, something happened between my grandmother and her siblings that caused a divide, the details of which we know nothing about. There are rumbling rumors which we can't decipher because none of us were there to witness. Now we have this apparent divide that no one seems to know how or care to reconcile. We can never achieve total family unity because of an infected body of relatives. Nobody will speak about the disagreement that caused the divide. People continue to dismiss it as if it does not exist. Yet the divide yields the symptoms of the longstanding psoriasis or virus, whichever is more shameful given that everybody claims they love family, and it's all academic. It's pure B.S.!! (uhmm — Bachelor of Science) The immediate family involved have since passed on, leaving the rest of the family without a vestige, vial, or a needle even; forget the vaccine! Lack of knowledge of the occurring event of casualty sets up no barriers leaving the family exposed and vulnerable to attacks of the enemy to perpetuate an already severed bond.

Families have perfected the art of talking at each other, which is highly effective communication — notttt — but the choice to disengage when there is no accountability or reconciliation is perplexedly understandable. It is not fair to anyone to try to coexist with those committed to dismissive and rude behavior. One's commitment to rude behavior then evokes the other person's right of disengaging. When the sanctity of family is in jeopardy, common ground can help to eliminate division. That level of love, forgiveness, and acceptance allows for reunification. Paul, as a Roman citizen, would call this reconciliation. It does family well to study the writings of Paul in the New Testament — so many similarities. Go figure! Maybe our families are the reason, as Christians believe, God sent his only begotten son to save generation after generation.

There is something about being hurt, mocked or alienated by family that deadens the desire to even want to be a part of that something greater than themselves, the organization called family. I mean, if family ain't family, why bother? The desire to take part becomes difficult in maintaining fellowship with the collective if all it does is showcase reasons why one does not fit into the box they prefer to keep you in.

I remember mamma used to tell me stories about how she and her siblings were told by their father not to fight amongst each other. He taught them to stand together and would tell them, "If one of y'all get into a fight, then all y'all get in the fight." She said that is how they got to be known as "Them Emerson Girls". There were seven total kids, six girls and one boy. They all were a beautiful mix of gentleness and rage, a group of beautifully flawed women who fought tooth and nail to protect their children from the cruelties of the world. Sometimes they may not have gotten it right, but that in no way negated the undeniable love amongst them. Being the youngest of all their children makes my position in the family unique. All my first cousins are at least ten to twenty years older than me. I am younger than some of their children, which makes for the funniest jokes sometimes.

It was said that I was to be the one to bridge the gap between the older and younger generations, and I am compelled to uphold that prophecy to the best of my ability. They may not all like me, and we may not speak, but I feel it is my duty to do what is right and civil by every family member, and nothing will change that charge I gave to myself. By no means are we perfect, and I have experienced my share of troubled waters, but when it comes down to the wire, they will never be far from the love I have to give. Rapids of troubled waters have come more often as of late, and I have spent a good portion of time feeling as though it is always me against the whole. Just like in all families, we have good and bad experiences, but one thing is for sure, in the time of trouble, they show up. There is always a faithful few that will show up for whatever, when and wherever.

There have been several experiences that warranted me to have to stand alone, and that, coupled with other experiences, made me question the genuineness of my acceptance by others. I know my delivery can come across less than the friendliest of ways. And when I speak, I speak in raw truth, but that does not deem me unlovable. We should do all things concerning the family collective decent and in order, I believe.

Because of the traumatic way in which I found my mother, someone concluded that I am now crazy. "Well, you know she found her mamma dead, so you know she crazy," were their words. But until one has physically, mentally and emotionally experienced such a shocking experience and tested their coping mechanism, speculation is inevitable, but no one can diagnose in a vacuum and speak about the sanity of one who has. We all have our crosses to bear, and that tree is mine and mine alone. It is simply not fair, inconsiderate, and ignorant to call me crazy even referencing such a traumatizing event for a teen child. And maybe I am by some psychological standard. My brain certainly experienced severe emotional trauma, and yes the pain lingers through flashbacks, and it isn't erased from my frontal lobe. Maybe I don't realise or exhibit it, but that's just highly insensitive and borderline cruel to say to someone, especially family.

I've even been called evil spirited. The running joke is that I am the evil uncooperative one, and that's because I will not do things the way others would have it. I like that though, because it means I can express my individuality and still respect myself enough to know I stayed true to what matters to me. If it wasn't people around me or strangers calling me mean, it was my family saying such things while throwing in a laugh to soften the blow. Years of hearing that raises the question, "Is that what they think of me, an evil uncooperative misfit?" Fighting against relatives over such things was so commonplace that fighting against the world became effortless. For others to think of me in this way because of the people who were assumed to love me the most used to bother me. It was just disheartening. The people I thought would love and protect me the most have exacted cruelty upon me and, so, are the ones who have hurt me worst.

A person who will not stand for anything, including what they believe is right and fair, will fall for anything, especially subtle, misguided manipulations. Despite whatever they think of me, I will stand firm on who I am and what I believe in, even if it means I must be a standalone, crazy, evil spirited, uncooperative, orrrrr naaaah. I will not in good faith go against what I believe is right just to appease the majority, nor will I compromise my own integrity to protect someone's manipulation, scare tactics, cruelty or insensitivity. Standing in the truth of what I believe does not make me any of the labels glued to the corrugate of my sanity and essence of being. Others' profiling my character is quite problematic, but my outer layer has experienced macro-evolution; I've transformed into teflon coated kevlar, frictionless and strong enough to manage that with ease. It's my defense mechanism which makes me unconditionally faithful to a standard that I hold sacred regarding the system of family. Unconditional love of family means being faithful to the honor code for the collective while standing against the honor code that benefits the ego even when the collective shifts, slipping into darkness. I have often felt alienated. It is not at all my intent to paint a perfect picture of myself, because I am flawed as well, so I learned to look at, evaluate, and temper how I address issues with my family.

Yes, I am honest and am quite ardent about what and how I feel, but there is always room for me to grow and learn how to better express myself without putting others on the defensive. I can recognize and acknowledge that within myself. However, it should not be acceptable to make me question my place or validity in the collective family simply because I ethically choose to do things in my own way which does not align with the way others deem necessarily preferable. They can say it, and it's true, I am mean. Some might say I am abrasive, but no one can say I didn't show up without question when my phone rang. Some actions made in the family will be genuine mistakes and others will be malicious intent used to cause disharmony. No matter how much anger ensues, one should never go against family, intending to inflict harm or emotional pain. Well, at least one might believe others will adopt that standard of thinking, but that is not always the case, and I have learned to accept when there are some who consciously resist sharing that sentiment. In giving people the space to be who they are, it means I give them the space to stand by and support whomever they so choose.

It is no longer a question of loyalty within family, but it begs the question of who they are loyal to. From personal experience, loyalty and allegiance is not always to family. Relatives have the freedom to stand by whomever they elect and for whatever reason. I have graduated to a place of comfort and acceptance with that. I cannot govern who a person places their allegiance to, but I can respect what they feel is the best thing for their lives by realising they have certain freedoms not to be restrained or disrespected. All one can do is accept it, respect it, and govern themselves accordingly. I will not allow someone's behavior to dictate how I show up when needed. I believe in the sanctity and unity of family, but I have had to learn that it is permissible and healthy to step back if those relationships are draining and unfulfilling.

The problem comes into play when most people are only looking for a handout instead of being a support system themselves. It is relevant because throughout the history of social media, it is commonplace to see comments or complaints of how the family has never shown up, but I would dare to inquire if the complainer was a 180° shift from the actual grievance. One should not expect what they are not willing to give. It seems people only want out of life and relationships what they can get for themselves with no additional thought about the scale of their willingness to give. The only time something is given is when opportunity arises to gain something in return. What if God thought the same way? That is the whole idea of family: To give, expecting nothing in return, given the presence of a special bond.

There should never be a time when a family does not support its own within his or her ability. In a perfect world, family bonds should be unbreakable. We should not compromise integrity within the family. Disloyalty or unfaithfulness should be at best fleeting thoughts. Family is precisely more about the integrity of the collective than it is about one individual. There is no dictatorship in the family unit. Of course, there is leadership, but the leadership role is about facilitating, ushering unity, and strengthening the established bond which may have existed for centuries.

The attitude of a genuine leader is to have an all-inclusive mentality. True leaders are careful not to alienate or set themselves apart from the majority. There is no big "I" and little "you" within the family collective. Unconditional family relationships should always be open and honest, even if being honest means speaking a truth that hurts. That truth speaks in a way that is amicable, and the recipient can process it without the misconception of ill intent.

Using the truth to hurt or embarrass someone is an ill-orchestrated devious plot to tear others down. Some things are hard to come back from after someone has a permanent bruise from the venomous words spewed or malicious actions effected. It is best to keep open lines of communication. Unconditional love of family does not alienate each other or make anyone feel unwelcome. Unconditional family relationships under no circumstances allow outside sources to dictate and or sow weeds of discord within the irrigated fields of the family collective lest the weeds choke out the crop. Even if discord permeates familial relationships with a ripple effect, that discord should be rounded up and weeded out by the affected unit for reconciliation and restoration of the relationship.

Accountability must be prevalent within unconditional family relationships. Transparency and reverence should govern in trust and acceptance.

I used to walk around with a cane of bitterness and resentment, and I had to ask myself, "Why am I so angry?"

I realise now that I held that anger because I expected a certain standard of behavior from others hopelessly fallen short, and when that behavior did not materialize, I harbored that disappointment in the craters of my heart. It later festered and became bitterness and resentment. It was then that the Holy Spirit whispered to me that I cannot expect righteousness from unrighteous people and that even I was unrighteous. Hearing and realizing this truth set me free from the crippled walk supported by that cane of bitterness and resentment. I soon realised that there are different levels of righteous behavior, and because someone does not reach the same level of growth or righteousness, it serves me no purpose to hold that bitterness in my heart, for none but one is righteous. *Matt 19:17 "No one is good but One, that is God." (NKJV)*

I cannot control a person's free will to behave as they see fit, just like I would want no one trying to control mine. A person's definition of righteousness depends a great deal on their perspective, experiences, and whom they serve. But, in determining what's comfortable for them within the moral will of God, no one has the right to preempt a person's will to do what he chooses and how he chooses to perform it. It's already ordained by God since it falls within His moral will. I don't need to hold on to bitterness or resentment because someone's moral choice differs from my own. It serves me no purpose to compare the acts of kindness of others against my own, especially when God attributes His righteousness to the believer by grace alone. It is my duty to best follow what I feel God lays on my heart to do.

There is always a choice to engage with others or not. That is where my ability to have grace resides. I released the negative energy that I had been carrying and moved forward in the strength of who I am. I understand and accept that people behave from their frame of reference and that reference has more to do with their experiences and nothing to do with my own experiences. My love does not and will never waiver, for it is the love of the divine. God gave me this heart, and despite the people who have wounded me on this journey called life, I make a conscious effort to continue to love as God commanded. I hope to have an earthly love that resembles the love of God. As I serve God and others, it is my duty to reflect the love of my creator to the best of my ability. Yes, there are days that I am tempted to not live and abide in that love, but I have found a certain level of peace in holding on to who I am and how I want to be perceived in this world. My love remains genuine, and my intention is always honorable.

I now know that not verbalizing feelings does more damage to the person holding on to unexpressed emotion than it does to anyone else. And it doesn't even matter if others receive what we have said. What matters most is that the individual finds the courage to express their feelings in ways that serve the greater good of everyone involved. That is freedom, and it releases destructive, negative energy one might carry stagnating within. There is value in speaking the truth of how we feel. It's not what you say, it's how you say it. It takes courage to stand in one's own truth and speak it. Speaking truth gives a person countless opportunities to move through the frustrations of unexpressed emotion with ease, opening the way for them to come out on the other side in peace. Acknowledging and understanding one's authentic feelings teaches the lessons needed for a person to better understand and know themselves, giving them the space to authenticate and actualize who they choose to be. Freeing oneself from harbored emotion is paramount because it is refreshing and invigorating. Holding on to emotional baggage keeps one from living life in the "free free" of who they are. It matters most that one loves themselves unconditionally, always chastening their intentions to remain pure. Living in that space keeps a person centered, at peace, and truly alive.

Within the family collective, a child's first friendships are with their siblings and cousins. It is amazing to have relatives that can be considered friends; that makes the relationship that much more special.

Understanding family dynamics is the premise of understanding familial relationships. It is in those first familial relationships one learns the art of friendship and forgiveness. It takes unconditional acceptance and love to move through the pain to find forgiveness in the heart. Your daily life-sized Instagram may not always draw likes, but there should always be authentic emoji hearts of love. Within a family unit, love is organic and accepting of everyone. Often people feel as though they are not accepted or respected, and that is why they decide to dissociate with other family members.

We must learn how to accept people as they are and be a light that they may see love clearly in the actions of everyone. The unique bond amongst families should be representative of storge love which withstands any attempt to weaken it to the point of collapse or brokenness. As individuals, our love may shift and stagger but should never wane to the point of perish.

A family system should be all-inclusive as a show of mutual love, respect, belonging, acceptance, and inheritance amongst the entire clan. In no way are the indiscretions of one person reflective of the character of the whole. To see it any other way is a misrepresentation and flaw in characterizing the heartbeat of the quality of family. For me, I struggled to fit in, to feel welcomed as part of my emotional inheritance. The ignorance of storge love prevailed with no enlightenment in sight, and I gave up trying. One day that desire to be part of the clan was permanently preempted by ignorance, distaste, and stoked emotions of outcast. As the odds of being accepted by certain relatives veered more heavily unfavorable, my demand for respect illuminated. It was fine in a sense that they chose not to accept me because the truth that no one could deny was that all I did was follow the laws of nature, exit my mother's birth canal. Because of ignorance and selfishness, my trip into this world colored my mere existence a threat. After so many years had gone by of not being included, the idea of reconciliation and acceptance became null and void, almost senseless. That fight was hard fought for many years until my volcanic emotions erupted in a manner that shook up the atmosphere. That explosion of emotion eased all the pent-up bitterness and unexpressed annoyances that I cratered as hot, molten discontent for years.

After enduring thirty years of blatant disrespect, my breaking point had come upon me like an earthquake and I was not at all remorseful. I was angry that it took me so long to walk along the fault line of emotional distaste and finally stand in my own power discontinuing subjecting myself to the emotionally abusive behavior of people who didn't even know my proper name. They are unworthy of another ounce of my energy.

I thought overlooking the ignorance of them was the way to prove how I felt about my father, but I have since learned that I don't have to subject myself to the abuse of anyone committed to being blind to the beauty of who I am and mistreating me because I was the by-product of an affair. So no, I don't regret setting myself apart from anyone who chooses not to give me an inherited right of inclusion. How can they hate a member of their own family with whom they have never had conversation? There is nothing comparable to the feelings of being deemed an outcast before you even step into a room. It is unjust to deem someone unworthy before you even know their name. How dare these people even for a minute allow themselves to believe that I was less deserving of love because they chose not to see the beauty of God's gift to the family circle. Counting me out and considering me undeserving of having an equal part or position in certain sectors of what most would call family is unthinkable. I have endured this rejection for way longer than I should have. It's a wonder my insanity hadn't surfaced with the emotional volcanic explosion.

Not one convincing word uttered effectively on my behalf by the ones who had the power to change the dynamic of the whole situation, thus allowing certain ones to dismiss my existence as if I were some stray they had found on the street is dehumanizing, unthinkable. I never spoke up about even subtle actions taken to ensure I understood I was not at all welcome within that collective. I remained silent because my father meant more to me than quashing the sheer ignorance of behavior towards me. Accepting that my birthright was repressed, even freedom of speech, and I don't mean my 1st Amendment right to speak, I just grinned and bared it. My mamma raised me to respect others, and I chose to not disrespect that environment. Instead, I allowed those feelings of exclusion to fester and gnaw away at my insecurities. I eventually unraveled as my tether weakened from the tattering caused by the malicious and constant gnaw, pulled apart and lost all tenacity of respect.

Now that I have spoken and released the negative energy of that toxic dynamic, the separation feels better. The heat of discontented lava escaped with my explosion, cooling as it created new ground for me to stand on. I told myself that it was fine because I was doing it for a greater good. So, for the sake of love, I endured sub-par treatment for years. I remember how lonely it felt to spend holidays surrounded by people and still being very much orphaned. To sit off alone in a corner while the rest of the circle laughed gave me the tools I needed to further detach and disconnect. I grew more and more numb at every gathering, for there was no interest in Roman adoption of even one of their own. I can tell you unequivocally that years of emotional abuse takes its due toll whether you're willing to pay it or not.

My biggest complaint is that I didn't realise the effect it was having on me in those moments. The resilience gave me what I needed to get past foolish behavior of immaturity and lack of self-love. I don't remember ever feeling de-orphaned, embraced or accepted, which caused me to retreat further into myself and my nonchalance. Those experiences designed for me the template of disconnect. Of course, playing the blame game would say that it was me that denied inclusion. Albeit highly plausible, I would rebut, "But nobody in their right mind would want to be a part of a group of people that regarded them as an outcast, an orphan just because I was my father's illegitimate child. Viewed as an alien, an extraterrestrial, an outsider from the beginning, how could I?" So there, I said it — illegitimate. I said it, but illegitimacy does not define me, nor does it define any of you. Millions of us are born out of wedlock and are some of the most accomplished worldwide, so there is no credence to any human being regarded as less deserving of love than another and being denied a birthright of inheritance, of belonging, period. I feel as though this goes without saying, but it sure doesn't feel that way in my dysfunctional family.

I can remember at sixteen or seventeen years old being at the beauty salon and sitting under the dryer, and no one in the room knew I could hear the conversations being had. It was those conversations that validated that they would never accept me. I heard the murmurs intended to prove that very notion and, in that moment, I sanctified myself, set myself apart because I knew I was unwanted. In that moment there could have been some confirmation that I have a rightful place in that family unit, but as time eventually told, not a word surfaced in support of full fledged admission of rights or adoption on my behalf. Hindsight once again taught me the truth in that there was never any actual attempt to include me. Being a 17 year old and to not only hear but feel that kind of dejection crushed my feelings beyond any kind of redeemable repair. That defining moment caused my membrane of protection to grow more expansively. To disregard my feelings and property only taught me on a deeper level that nor I or the things I cared about were of any concern to them.

I paid the price of indiscretion without taking possession of ownership. While I no longer hold any ill-feelings nor ill-will towards anyone or about anything, I maintain that they could have made better provisions for me. But I understand; one cannot give what they themselves never received. I suffered resentment for indiscretions that drove a wedge that not even time could rot away, and I bore the weight of that burden far too long. It was easier to target me than confronting the actual issue. I find no value in casting blame on anyone; what is done is done, and there is nothing that can change that fact, even with an unconditional commitment to not accept those disliked the most. Maturity should have been a factor to influence better decisions, but when one operates from a loathsome place of being, wisdom to do what is noble, fair, and honorable withers, whittling down to kindness unrecognizable. It was readily apparent that God had not blessed my family as a whole with profound wisdom or tolerance.

Still, no real reason to detest my existence has been nor can ever be validated by anyone, probably because there is no such rule or law in the universe that legislates such demonic behavior. I just learned to not feel any inclination to force myself into situations where I knew I was not welcome. Those experiences taught me to be ok with alienation from others. That was a valuable lesson to learn. It equipped me with the authority to stand in crowded rooms and remain true to my very essence. I learned how not to conform to the crowd and remained true to my own convictions. I never want to be that person who abandons her own belief system for gregarious acceptance. Humans will abandon anything to get the praise and acceptance they seek. That is an accurate definition of "sell out." They sell their own souls to gain validation from people in the crowd who don't even know nor are happy with themselves. For what does it profit a person to gain acceptance of the world and lose the integrity of their own soul. (Similarly stated in Matt 16:26 NKJV)

To the misled, I am a constant reminder of a blemish that shall never fade, no matter the effort to scrub it clean — eliminating my presence altogether. Perhaps they act out their mother's resentment of my mother or me for that matter. It would explain the truth that I have been tolerated instead of actually accepted. I have learned to overlook blatant ignorance of anyone who knows nothing about where I have been or who I believe myself to be. Alienating me became a seen and unseen practice for the duration. I understand and accept that there are degrees of love among relatives and family that depends a good deal on shared experiences. There is a different love that exists among those who share a lifetime of memories and experiences versus those that attach later in life. Love is neither necessarily bad nor good, rather it boasts different degrees of intensity. That has been an indirect battle I have had to fight since my mother's departure.

It is comforting to know and feel at least that my sister and husband and big brothers stood up for me. And, of course, my daddy has always expressed his love for me. I love you Daddy, always. As for my big brother, always showing up for "baby girl" as he calls me, I have been calling on him my whole life. He always comes running, whether coming from across town to remove a dead frog that's stuck to my garage or cutting down trees in my backyard. He was cutting this tree down for me, and I was standing there holding back tears (cause I'm a big baby), but it didn't take much to make me cry — lol. I was tearful 'cause I'm grateful to him and my big sister. They take care of me. And I just hope that I have loved them by my actions and not just my words. Mamma taught us all how to be servants in all her selfless acts.

Perplexedly, there were those who refused to accept me, yet, there were others standing in solidarity to at least acknowledge my existence and frame of reference, but it was not fair to continue to allow those particular supporters to suffer the repercussions of undue stress, dealing with the opposition because of their support for me.

As I am days away from declaring the gestational period of this work, my father's wife was just called away from this earth, unexpectedly. May her soul rest in peace and my father and his family find solace and mercy under God's wings.

For them, I am forever grateful for those who exercised their ability to see me, hear and feel my heart, and to act under the color of mutual love and respect. They extended an olive branch of love, peace and inclusion by choice when they too could have swept me aside. It is those additional relationship which also deserve honor and proliferation — my supporting brothers and their significant others. As many negative experiences and people that I have encountered in my lifelong journey, that faithful few, never wavered in their love for and embrace of me. So when I say not a word uttered on my behalf, they are included in context, but not in reality, if that makes sense. It's as if they were threatened to keep silent, not outwardly expressing their disdain for the ill behavior of those who refused to accept me. The tenacity of my support base to unconditionally show love for me beyond the cliquish family circle carried me through the rough patches. Growing up, while in my immature and gullible state, most things only slightly affected me, but hindsight renders clearer perspective on unflattering situations that I could not see in real-time. It is quite clear where I stood and where I stand, and I have no desire to change my position. It is equally clear where they stand as well, and ungrudgingly, I realise and accept that the blind will never see me nor accept me. So, I am at peace with that revelation.

The day my mother left this realm, my sense of storge love dissipated right along with her. That experience robbed me of my sense of security and well-being. It has taken me years to retrieve that feeling. My inability to rest because I didn't feel protected stems from that trauma. With gratitude, I appreciate having had someone to step in and allow love to transcend any hardship and keep my physical well-being protected. I kept the sanctity of my heart off limits, out of reach, accessible to no one. I had it tucked way out of sight to keep it safe from even threat of harm. There were often times feelings of a bit of a love-hate tug of war were pervasive in my familial relationships: You know, when you want to believe that love is present, but you catch someone looking at you in disgust. That kind of tug of war eats away at the spirit and often reminds me that nor I or my feelings were obligatory. It sometimes felt as though I owed this enormous debt to a society that I would spend a lifetime trying to repay.

Those are the moments that made me feel unwanted or unloved the most. I think, maybe, repeated experiences put me in the mindset of always needing approval. Nothing I did seemed good enough. I have lived and taken part in that low vibrational state for most of my life. There was a time when I was free to just enjoy the moment, but experiences have taught me to sit down and fade into the background. That created a narrative in my mind that says anytime I step outside the box, I am attention seeking, so it snares me and makes me afraid to set myself free, but the faded reflection in the mirror is screaming at me to break free from the chains of that narrative that may not have been my own. That reflection reminds me that I create and control my own narrative and that I am free to operate outside of any box that someone places me in for any reason, including their fears and/or insecurities.

I have experiences with those who will give you all the love they can as long as you don't challenge the conditions of their love, or should I say intent or manipulations. Avoid becoming the footstool of someone who wishes to undermine your experiences while expanding their own. There are some who will attempt this because of their underlying need to feel more important which stems from unexpressed insecurities. It is easier to minimize the experience of someone else while exaggerating one's own insecurities as confidence instead, because admitting insecurity seemingly is a sign of weakness. It's that person who wants to see you happy, just not happier than them. They want to know you are doing big things, just not bigger than them. If we are not careful, we could spend our entire life in a box imagined by others, ignorant or not, who desire to keep us trapped in with root cause stemming from their own insecurities. Expand and contract your personality on an as needed basis; concrete does, and it's very secure with maybe a few hairline cracks here and there. Not everyone deserves the beauty of your authenticity, especially when they try to box you up and keep you tucked away until they feel the need to let you out and play. I've experienced this where the persons became bored and were just in need of something or someone to manipulate. It is ludicrous to afford one's notoriety on the dismissal of another.

Storge, familial or born of friendship, you are worthy to be loved, included, respected, an heir to the inheritance of your birthright. Though you can't force even family to love you, you can pray for the strength to handle the senseless dejection and vow never to treat a human being as some of us have been mal-treated. You are special. Face the person looking back at you, reflecting all that you are and all that you desire to be. Don't be afraid of the raw truth staring through your eyes into your soul.

Earlier, I asked the question, "Why is it that we can't face the truth of who we are?"

I say to that, "Why would I ever include myself in that class of cowards? Yes, cowards. Cowardice is the instigator of hiding one's face to spare self the truth of who we are. I own who God created me to be, and I will seek my Highest Good until it is crystal clear to me that I have achieved all that I desire and that He desires for me.

Regardless of the currents and troubled tides of trues, I can shatter the faded reflection in the mirror and realise my breakthrough, rowing safely to the other side of beauty, felicity and success. I shall remain on course traversing this nautical route until 'The Bitter End.'"[31]

---

[31] Relates to The Bitter End Yacht Club in the British Virgin Island's Virgin Gorda, decimated by Hurricane Irma in 2017. The Bitter End is in close proximity to Saba Rock and privately owned Neckar Island, owned by billionaire, Richard Branson, founder of Virgin Atlantic Airlines Limited and Virgin Atlantic International Limited, Virgin Mobile, and Virgin Records. From Saba Rock's pier where you dock your 42 foot sail boat, Catamaran, etc., you can lower your dingy and ride the waves to both The Bitter End and Neckar island. The trauma inflicted upon the beautiful Virgin Islands will find healing, repair, and strength through God's grace, as will you and I.

Self-Check

What do you need to accept about yourself that would prohibit you from standing in the genuine power of who you are?

_____

_____

_____

_____

_____

_____

What box have you allowed yourself to be kept in because of someone else's insecurities?

_____

_____

_____

_____

_____

_____

7 unKonditional
RELATIONSHIP

Our need of belonging is sponsored by human nature.

Relationships cannot survive one sided, unbalanced effort. They survive when there is an equal effort applied where every party is committed to making the relationship meaningful. It is not at all about fulfilling the needs of only one person in the relationship but catering to the needs of all parties. Relationships are about connections. Once a person masters their relationship with self, they should become more open to connect with others. For it is that connection that establishes foundation in the relationship. It is a partnership where both individuals service each other to create balance, eliminating polarity within the connection. By making the needs of the other person priority, both prime the relationship for success. Selfishness does not live within the domain of a relationship. There should be no intention for one to lose their individuality, for it is the meshing of two individuals which makes the whole. Individuals will find it advantageous exercising their true capacity to maintain their individuality. It is counterproductive to lose any part of oneself in a relationship. A person should not allow others to treat them as if to invalidate them or their feelings.

Ideal relationships are about learning how to complement and support each other in every way. They need not be as hard as society has conditioned most to believe, so long as there is open communication and consent of those involved. By whose standards have we deemed relationships hard? Here again, do we believe relationships are hard because we have tried and failed, or do we believe that because someone told us that is what we should believe? It should not be difficult to maintain good relationships when individuals commit to trusting and being trustworthy. Often times, we fall in love with the idea of a person rather than the reality of who and what we see. Without even realizing it, we get this whole idea of what we expect in our head and end up overlooking the reality right in front of us. In personal relationships, we must bare the nakedness of who we are and what we need, and partners must accept the who and what we bare. That is where healthy compromise emerges. The fear of rejection prevents us from embracing and expressing the truth of who we are, and what they need within the perimeter of relationship. Honest connection and communication breeds mutual compromise.

For two personalities to coexist in a relationship, one must know when to expand or contract in certain situations. There will be instances where one person will be stronger at a thing than the other and vice versa. And so, one complements the other. Relationships are not about fitting into specific classes and remaining stagnated in that persona of who and what one should be. It is about either person having the ability to lead and sometimes follow. Partnerships are where the individuals can find common ground in most everything. It can become problematic if a person is too dominating in nearly every area of the relationship. Every individual in any relationship has a need to feel as if they belong. No matter the scenario, no matter the space, our need of belonging is sponsored by human nature. They also desire to feel wanted and appreciated, but mostly they need to feel valued. We are created to be in relationships, so we should make the best effort to coexist. It is within those relationships that people need to feel worthy, be seen, and be heard. They must be willing to be vulnerable to the people closest to them.

I believe that most people walk around so afraid to show vulnerability that they wear this mask as if they don't need anyone or anything. The faded reflections in their mirror have not yet revealed that all people need someone. The ego is persistent in the ideal that people don't need each other. We lie to ourselves for fear of being hurt. No one wants to feel that pain, but pain unfortunately is an unavoidable experience of our existence. There is no way of avoiding it. In the grand scheme of things, no one wants to feel as if they are standing in the shadows of the person they are in relations with. So, there are some instances when it is beneficial to adjust within the relationship so that both individuals are ultimately at peace. The willingness to make specific compromises suggests that both individuals are comfortable enough to say how the relationship progresses. Healthy relationships consist of healthy communication.

Healthy communication is respectful, open, honest, and is best had when neither individual is guarded. It does not put the other person on guard, nor does it make them feel emasculated in any way. Healthy communication influences unity and does not incite separation. It is not boastful or prideful. It is laced with humility and thoughtfulness. It is believable that anyone can understand anything if there is an honest conversation that takes place. Open and honest communication without any threat of lies and deceit are essential in a successful relationship. Communicating desires and finding common ground for compromise is the best way to maintain a relational ease. It is those things that are conducive to maintaining relationships. Toxic free relationships increase happiness while creating a steady flow of peace. Being supportive of each other is instinctual. Successful relationships are ones where individuals are willing to learn how to connect on meaningful levels.

With this new wave of social media, people have lost the ability to relate or connect with one another. Social media has taught people the art of disconnect within their relationships. Most have lost the skills needed for successful interpersonal interaction. Without interpersonal interaction, the opportunity for connection with anyone is void of possibility. It is a construct of the ego to think and believe that we don't need to connect to others to gain some fulfillment. The soul yearns for unity, and with unity comes connection. Both individuals should have a desire to work to maintain mutual respect and honest interaction, regardless of circumstances. Good relationships are bound to have hiccups. No relationship is free of turbulence, but the key is to be able to buckle up, stay calm, and stabilize, reaching a compromise amicably. There will be problems that arise, but it is how those problems are approached that will determine the facilitation of resolve.

Compromise is essential in unconditional relationships, helping each person better to feel safe enough to voice their desires without verbal or suggestive repercussion. They are saturated with mutual respect. Disagreements do not have to be a detriment to relationships and should not automatically signify termination. They present an opportunity for both parties to gain a deeper understanding of the other person. Deeper understanding influences the evolution of the relationship into deeper levels of love and connection. The more both individuals know and truly understand about the other person, the better the provision for them to have a lasting as well as loving relationship. Disrespect only produces extreme levels of toxicity in relationships. Disagreements will occur, and that is why it is always better to understand effective ways to handle them when they arise. Unhealthy relationships are riddled with neglect and inundated with selfish behavior. One should not neglect their own needs to please the needs of another. That is not a balanced and interactive relationship. It is not at all fair, nor is it justified. It only increases the selfishness of the individual in the relationship. Mental, emotional, and physical neglect in relationships is, in many facets, considered abusive. Abuse on all levels is intolerable and unacceptable. There is, however, a balance between selfless and taking care of self first.

The faded reflection in my mirror has shown me that expressing my angry feelings explosively is not effective communication. Expressions of such intensity only compels the other individual to lose interest and most times desire as well. The faded reflection taught me that there are better ways to get my point across without the added aggression in my words and tone. I realise that in some ways my aggression emasculates the other person and renders them unwilling to engage. I had to learn how to control my anger, something that is still very much a struggle for me, especially because I have lived most of my days feeling like I am not heard.

It is my softness that is more powerful than my rage. That rage rendered me hopeless in moments when I really needed for my words to be heard. The key to effective communication would be for me to contract, pull back in those situations and not match the energy in the room. My softness in this setting is more powerful than my aggression. I had to learn to soften my communication, even in moments that I felt dismissed and undesirable.

The mirror showed me that operating in the fullness of my femininity meant that I needed to deflate the aggressive energy when it flares up or flares are shot entering my space triggering my own aggression. It works better to shift my energy and counteract the aggression while at the same time disarming it. It is not at all an easy lesson to learn, because when I am mad, I really want to snap, crackle, and pop, but if I want to be heard, I have to shift my energy and become the "effective communicator," taking the high road to calm and resolve.

When I am mad, I want to express my genuine anger. Anger is a valid emotion, so I don't understand why I should have to tiptoe around those angry emotions. Truth is, I just no longer want to be that person who blows up when I'm angry. I wanted to disarm my aggression and learn to use softness so as not to emasculate anyone. The disarming of aggression allows for everyone to be heard and valued even in situations of dispute. Within the partnership, both individuals create safe spaces to express vulnerabilities. If I wanted to make relationships last, I had to let go of my methods of expressing my anger because it was clearly proven ineffective. Just like I didn't want to be the receiver of aggression, I had to learn to better express myself in ways to lessen my aggression as the offender.

i. Romantic Relationships

Trust is a very necessary layer in the foundation of a relationship. Without trust, it's all fluff that turns to dust. There is no relation, and the ship will inevitably set sail without it. Relationships are subject to serious breakdown absent the lubricant of trust. The types of love which fall into this class are Eros, Ludus, Pragma, and, narrowly, Mania.

Shareholders in relationship with each other will build a substantial trust if they want to be successful in growing, maturing and protecting their investment. That means inserting trust in the entire portfolio entrusting each other with the deep and possibly darkest parts of themselves, not just the glaringly apparent winning stocks and attributes. Keep in mind that not everyone deserves access to that portfolio of intimacy because the wrong person will take that treasure chest of vulnerability and weaponize it to vanquish you and all that you're vested in. I'd be most concerned with Mania, the obsessive and possessive in this regard. But that level of intimacy with the right person is what is going to help that relationship thrive.

If that kind of trust is not present, the relationship has a foundation of sand to rest on and will surely crumble in turbulent weather. Feeble, unsettling foundations do not sustain relationships effectively. The chances of growth diminish when trust is not present. Trust and acceptance are pertinent in all relationships. One must be willing to accept the other person fully to achieve that level of intimacy.

ii. Eros

Lover of the body — Romantic love. It was termed by the Greek as sexual attraction, intimacy between two people. It is named for the Greek god of love and sexual desire, Eros. This love is passionate and full of desire spawned from a catalyst of physical attraction aesthetically, hormones, pheromones, and even aphrodisiacs. The word erotic derives from Eros. You know Eros' Latin counterpart as Cupid. Yep, the guy that has a quiver filled with love laced arrows. Maybe he's pierced your heart a time or two. He even did it to himself, or so the myth goes, after which, he falls for an incredibly gorgeous woman who rivals Venus, and that messes with Venus' psyche. Coincidentally, this goddess-like woman who is attracting all the attention and is the talk of the town goes by the name of none other than — Psyche. How convenient!

The life lessons that are to be learned depend a great deal on the psyche of the individual. I have not had much success with relationships, not from a lack of trying, but I think the trauma of losing my mother and the distant nature of my father due to his infidelity with my mother created an irreparable disconnect within me that I just never could solder back together. I know, I've heard it used to describe me before, and you may be thinking that same thing right now, "damaged goods." Just as Venus developed a complex about Psyche, I did the same with my ordeal. I choose not to run from this term, rather I embrace it because I stand a greater chance of repair. Recognizing the condition in the terms that others label you is a brave first step to wellness. I own that state of being without criticizing and belittling myself. Acknowledging can go one of two ways, however, north or south. I choose north. I had become increasingly aware of my feelings of disconnect not only from other people but from myself as well. I could not understand how it was that a person could disconnect within themselves, but it is in fact the reality of how I felt.

The faded reflection prompted me to ask myself why I never had any successful relationships. That question caused me to take pause. I then took a Ginsu knife and exacted an incision of authority into my past, peeled back a layer daringly, and introspectively gathered and analyzed data. I connected the dots carefully and began to produce information. That information led me to the conclusion that the facts were crystal clear and undeniable. Facing the facts was another tough and brave choice. The facts established that I was the common denominator in all my failed relationships, which now was proof that the issue lay within me, not other people. But why was there an issue, and what was it that took root and manifested to sabotage my ability to have lasting relationships?

So again, I made an exacting incision into my past and peeled back another layer for even deeper introspection. I wondered if, somehow beneath all the layers, I would uncover and recognize a root of connectivity to the upper layer. I saw complicated relationships and flings covered by complex feelings and twisted emotions with identical broken hearts strewn in the vicinity of every relationship. The sight of this misery caused me to quiver, and I became a bit queasy. And, in that moment, I covered my mouth and clutched my stomach and bent forward. Given that which I diagnosed, the feeling gushed forth that I was undeserving of love. I am not sure if somewhere in the back of my mind I hadn't stored this thought or verdict for quite a long time that I just didn't deserve love at all.

The truth from the faded reflection revealed that I felt like no one would love me back. Then the question became, "When and where did I start believing that lie?"

So with another quick incision of authority, I peeled back yet another layer. It must have come from the stories I had been telling myself, and over time, those stories took root and became my status quo. Once it became ingrained into my subconscious as a core belief, it was inevitable that those would be the kind of experiences that I would subconsciously attract. I now know that I am very much deserving of love and respect. My flaws in no way deem me unworthy of love, for my flaws do not define my character. I didn't always live with that belief, but somehow it had been embedded into my subconscious and had become a part of how I thought about relationships. I figured out the root cause of that belief, and it was the result of me loving someone and love not being returned. That experience unfortunately set the blueprint for most of my experiences from then on. Because love was not returned in that experience, I told myself and believed that no one would ever love me back and that belief took root.

Some would say or believe that my issues in romantic relationships stem from issues with my father, but I have not been able to make that connection. I have no disbelief in my father's love for me. I realise that my father was a man before he became my father, and that means that he would certainly make some mistakes, don't we all? But that hardly equates to him not being there for me. He has never not been there when I needed him most, but the truth of the matter is that I always felt like I was on the other side of the railroad tracks of his family. I don't ever recall having been included as or felt a part of his family. I have always been on the outside looking in. For obvious aforementioned reasons, it's not difficult for one to reason why I have never fully been embraced.

I probably will never understand that reasoning because I am not the one at fault, but that's just society acting out regarding an act that has always been taboo, a cardinal sin. It's certainly unfortunate and maybe even understandable, but being on the outside of the fence, I think differently because I feel in full effect what it's like to be dejected due to the other side's trained emotional reflex. And, undoubtedly, it's a complex emotion that is hard to reverse unless you've been the illegitimate seed gasping for the heir of love and acceptance.

What's worse for me, though, is that, somehow, God saw fit for me to have to carry that burden with my mamma's passing. So, I will not waste another moment of my life trying to figure it out. It just is, and I promise that I will never treat or subject a child to the estrangement that I have so brutally endured. We must see human beings in the light that we all need and desire unconditional love and acceptance. And even if societal traditions, rules, dogmas and principles do not agree that we deserve such treatment situationally dependent, grace absolutely must prevail if we intend on receiving grace from the Father.

I have come to accept and understand that both my parents are individuals that are products of the flesh and their own trauma, so I don't hold any grudge or ill feelings toward them for the way they chose to live their lives. Accepting that truth makes it easy for me to extend grace and understanding that they were indeed flawed but did what felt good to them at the time. The principle of "Greater Good," would take issue with this, but again, the flesh is weak, and it's a flaw they chose to entertain. Yet, there is no amount of criticism or pronouncement of this trauma that will ever disconnect my father from the love I hold for him. In his own imperfect way, he showed me how not to live inside a box. In a lot of ways, I am just like him. My mamma would always tell me, "You got 'pop eyes' just like your daddy." That always made me smile, even now when I hear her say it.:-)

The amazing thing about experiences is that there is something to be learned whether good, bad, or indifferent. I gave my all to someone, and when love was not returned, that experience taught me that I, at my best, wasn't good enough. It made me believe that no one would ever love me back, and for years I have carried that in my spirit. I have always been afraid that I would never find anyone to love me back, and I questioned it every time I got close to thinking that someone showed interest. I never even considered that maybe there were other reasons that love returned void, reasons that I just couldn't see at the time. I instantly blamed myself. I didn't understand that another person's inability to return love had nothing at all to do with me, but everything to do with them.

Regardless of opportunities to have a bonafide romantic relationship, I always reserved a patch of topsoil for that seed to be planted, frustrating every one of my relationship experiences until I finally peeled back those layers and weeded out the tares from the root. Enough was too much as that seed planted was infectiously destructive my entire adulthood. That "enough" is terminated, yanked from the root because of ownership of the potential problem, the authority of introspection, and the bravery to seek out and vanquish root cause.

iii. Emotional Exfoliation Prep

Scribe and Strike Methodology

Repression of ill-emotions can be daunting and terrifying, and it can also consume lots of energy taxing the psyche dragging you in—to the black hole of mental instability. Traumatic feelings have a way of confusing life for the affected, and so preparation for dealing with emotional trauma is a must. Emotions detrimental to the physical and mental health and wealth of a victim takes time to repress. You realise this when thoughts and feelings of regret and even fear are recurring, especially when not being properly addressed with a qualified physician or therapist. It just doesn't go away on its own, and neither is it wiped away with an etch-a-sketch overnight. Curing the symptoms may not be possible, but containing them can certainly be a reality if approached in logical stages. Exfoliation of these emotions require preparation, and that means you must be able to allow yourself to access the troubling emotions and scribe them, write them down, speak them out of you, declaring that they have no control, no power over you. This is a critical step whether seen by a therapist or not. I call this step the Scribe and Strike step, preparation methodology for deep

Emotional Exfoliation, the cleansing process of deep emotional trauma, and, that, we will discuss at great length in a later chapter.

This is how I now deal with my deep emotional trauma, "deep for deep." I held on to hope that he would see that I was the one for him, but of course he never came to that realisation. I allowed myself to be in that unfulfilling experience for way longer than I should have. Hindsight clearly illuminates that I erred in entertaining and putting up with a lot of things way longer than I should have. The time came when I had to accept the hard truth and just let it go. He would never see the beauty of who I was, and that had nothing to do with me. Certain situations made it undeniably clear that this just was not going to happen the way I had so desperately hoped, and I had no other alternative but to surrender to the truth of that situation and free myself from the anguish it was causing.

The interesting thing, though, is that while I hold no ill feelings toward that individual, the triggers from that experience still govern my thoughts and behavior. It has not been easy to unlearn and release the impact those triggers have on my mindset.

So, you're probably wondering why I continue to bombard you with my tragic familial and romantic experiences, but to many of you it sounds familiar. You are probably confused as to whether enough was enough and whether I've truly uprooted the problem and forged ahead. Funny thing you should contemplate. I feel like I just need to vent. I feel as if the only way I can definitively state that it's over is if I can write no more about the downside of the experiences. So, I'm expelling my pain through the imaginary ink in this *e*-pen, reaching out to you for support and to reciprocate because we all need a support base. And even though that base should forever be established with family, we know that that's not always the case in our dysfunctional worlds. Therefore, I am soliciting new, worthy friends and supporters who may have experienced something traumatic enough to send you close to or over the deep end seeking a lifeline. So with you in mind, I'm striking the next several lines which I have written to prove that you can do the same through universal love while listening, in spirit, to my personal theme song, "Pieces of Me," by the talented Ledisi, because I am, as is music, "You!niversal."

Though I am a unique individual, I am not an individual with a unique set of circumstances, rather an individual with a "You!nique" set of circumstances, for I am "You!niversal," I am You![32]

So let's strike these thoughts together! You will revert back after striking. That's Ok, simply release it, write to the contentment of your heart, and strike again as often as you need. Then be sure to speak uplifting words over your life. It's an iterative process of deep emotional exfoliation.

~~I have felt and actually been abandoned in nearly every relationship I have attempted. I felt that I wasn't good enough to be loved and, therefore, longevity of personal relationships have been as mystical as Pegasus or the Tooth Fairy. I allow manipulation because I am afraid to lose people in my life. I lost my mom, my rock, my protector, my everything so early in life. God chose that she would abandon me at nearly 14 years old. My father's family did all but right out reject me altogether. I felt so belittled, so dejected, so alone and helpless. Naturally, I allowed my thoughts about myself to be altered by those who just were not willing and ready to experience what I was ready to experience at the respective time. I should not have let that change who I was and how I thought about myself, but I fell prey. The abilities or inabilities of the person(s) of the moment had no reflection on who I was or will ever be, but I allowed those thoughts to spill over into what I thought all people would think about me. No one should give away that much of their own power to someone else. My feelings of abandonment lurked deep within me undetected, yet creating trauma at~~

---

[32] Trionfo, Victor (Alias), Editor in Chief, You!niversal You!nique, 2021

~~both the yin and the yang level. Call it a void, call it chaos, call it an implosion of destruction clandestine. I suffer from PTSD.~~

~~I gave what I wanted in return during intimate relationships but was never able to get to the next level. I realised the game was to keep women holding on to hope so that they would keep giving their all while receiving little to nothing in return. Yet, my fear of demolition abandonment kept me at bay. If a woman believes a man is going to measure up to the potential she sees in him, she will pretty much give everything she can to make it work. I fell in love with potential more times than I care to count. I used to think, if he would just open his eyes and see, he would see that I am "the one," but his eyes remained "wide shut" or maybe in all my relationships, I just was not the one. It felt like I was ghost, couldn't be seen. Truth is that men know whether they want to pursue something real, and they let women know by the things they say and the way they behave. I gave them opportunity to get what they wanted from me without them having to give back. Yeah — Hmmm — they capitalized on it.~~

So there, I did it! You can too! The pattern I recognized within myself is that I would always get so hung up in the potential for love that I would lose sight of the reality of what I was being shown. In that sense, my eyes, due to a physiological and psychological impediment, my eyes remained "wise shut." Yes, I meant to say that — wise shut. I lacked the wisdom to protect gullible me. I didn't think enough of myself, my beauty, my awesome strengths, my abilities to attract goodness to even remove the scales from my own eyes. How then could I expect them to. For those I saw potential with, I would give more hoping to receive the same in return. It wasn't much different with my own father's children. I am so done with that! I am distantly removed from that now, and thanks to these scribe and strike exercises, emotionally, I am on an incline. I am no longer stymied by the fear of demolition abandonment. "Eyes wide and wise shut." Cancelled!

That was my toxic trait! And that was the trait that certainly needed to be exfoliated. **Scribe — Strike — Scribe — Strike!**

I just exfoliated my toxic thoughts! I feel like shouting for joy, screaming from the top of a city building, making a scene! I am truly invigorated, and I feel powerful! I feel free! I may have lost my innocence in realisation, but that loving, carefree, positive energetic, hopeful me is back! I thank all of my You!niversal supporters in advance; Curtsy to all you survivors bravely actuating, emotionally exfoliating by taking hold of your frustration by the root and ending its destruction. Having done this once is not enough, though. It's an iterative process, so you will need to practice this daily until all the weeds are uprooted.

I never make a scene, except for this and one other time, lol, but we will not discuss that here. I am supposed to be trying to encourage you, the You!niverse, not expose my foolish, childish behavior, lol again.

Now back to "the rest of the story" – like I said, it's an iterative process, and you must train your mind to focus on the positive and strike the negative. The Law of Attraction would be happy with me right now.

iv. The Law of Attraction (Word frequency)

The law of attraction states that whatever the mind focuses on will manifest. Energy flows where the mind goes. It is possible that the "how" can affect what is envisioned, but one must not allow that question to block the flow of what is to come. It is best to focus on the positive outcome and trust the infinite one who controls the universe to orchestrate how it will appear. Relinquishing control is an extremely difficult task, but the law of attraction gives faith that letting go is necessary. Belief and trust are the foundation of this law. Whatever one believes wholeheartedly is what will manifest. Focusing on a desired outcome is what is bound to show up with the practice of patience and fearlessness. The more one focuses on things that go wrong in life, the more likely manifestation is more of the same. Experiences and ideas create belief, and whatever one believes is manifested in their reality. Becoming aware of what is believed consciously, subconsciously, and understanding how it creates one's reality is unbridled power. Understanding those beliefs that do or do not work is the work that one does to change their reality. Because we are energetic beings, who we are, and what we think vibrate out at certain frequencies.

There is a frequency for whatever one emits. Positive thoughts vibrate out at higher frequencies. The more one thinks on positive and uplifting things, the more they will attract positive outcomes. The same for those who vibrate on lower energy frequencies, they will attract back to them that which they vibrate out. A reason that this law becomes problematic is because one spends too much time trying to figure out "how" things will work out. The "how" should not be the concern of the individual. It is the concern of God, He who controls the universe. If we could dispel the myth that we must know every detail, we can begin to attract the desired outcomes along with attracting ways to make the outcomes happen. It is about learning to let go, trust, and have patience that the universe will manifest what we desire, even if it's raw love.

v. When Love Prevails

When I really cared, I would overextend myself only to be humiliated and alone in the end. I later learned how not to make a scene, I would just pick up the shattered pieces of my little bruised ego and move right along. Either way, it took years for me to see that it was just not going to happen and as hurtful as it was, the time came when I found the courage I so desperately needed to enable me to see, understand, and accept my truth. I guess that the time it takes for any of us to find the courage to step outside of what causes us pain varies per individual and the full and relevant circumstances. What matters is that we do find courage and exercise it boldly and gracefully. One does not have to be rude and attention seeking when standing in the power and truth of who we really are, performing what's necessary for the Highest Good of self. Being loud and boisterous is not the same as self-love standing in its power, owning one's total truth and unapologetically living out loud according to what one believes concerning truism for his or her own life.

I have found in my life that I hold on to situations that desperately needed letting go of because I didn't want to feel the pain of loss. I don't like to feel like I lost anyone, yet my affliction orchestrated that time and again. The trauma of losing the greatest person in my life put me in a frame of mind of never wanting to feel that hurt again. The irony of it is that my state of being guaranteed the exact opposite. I am so glad that I am finally able to understand that and can make better choices in the future. That faded reflection in my mirror is undeniably a great assistant of my healing. It is the universal law of attraction. That which we focus the most on is what we attract. I tried so hard to hold on to people that it became an anthem to prove that I could have and hold on to relationships. The deeper truth is that I needed to prove to myself that I could have and hold on to love because I didn't believe I could.

I needed to prove to myself that I was worth keeping because, at my core, I didn't believe I was good enough to be kept. Through all the layers of my own feelings of not being good enough, it became impossible for me to ask for what I needed. Because I had already told myself I wouldn't be granted my needs, afraid, I felt there was no need to ask. I settled into that clay for years. That sums up the complexity of my personality because most would consider me very outspoken, but in some situations, I won't open my mouth to even yawn. Funny how some things are not difficult at all to express, but asking for what I needed rendered me null and void of speech. This mix of extroversion and introversion accurately depicts my personality.

So, when the opportunity for love presented itself again, I thought, this time I am going to do things differently so that I can get a different result, but in hindsight, I was just doing more of the same. I was telling myself one story, still falling in love with potential and creating the familiar atmosphere of living the same old reality of love not being returned, and I didn't want to see the error of my ways. But this time, love gave me the courage to face myself. Love challenged me to be better and opened my eyes to a lot of things around and within me. Love, in a sense, removed the scales from my eyes and windexed my pupils so that i was endowed with the clarity of sight and the discernment of wisdom to interpret. It showed me with "Eyes wide Open" parts of myself that I didn't know existed. I am forever grateful to love for its existence. Love forced me to grow and change my perspective in many ways. Love showed me the opposite of who I had been, and I had to learn to be okay living the gray areas of life. Love gifted me with "Eyes wise Open" giving me the wisdom of discernment to realise that everything is not always black and white. It is not always going to be rainbows and green pastures. Love has ignited in my soul a truth and peace that surpasses even the comprehension of the inner trenches of my own mind. Love has freed me from the enslavement of my own pain. I can only hope that I can heal love in return. Love ignites within me an acceptable balance of love and hate.

Love and I are energetically and soulfully connected. It floods my soul with creativity. My authentic self is not afraid to give and receive when love is present. Love birthed in me a desire to reconnect to my own passion, thereby making it easier for me to connect with others. The journey back to me has been tedious, yet rewarding. Love gave me the confidence I needed to stand in my power and disengage from the distractions that offered no service to my higher good. Journeying home to oneself is a road less traveled for a reason. It's not for the faint at heart, the timid, the fearful, the aloof. Through love, I found the strength to stand in all my convictions even if it meant standing alone. Standing in my own conviction gives me the capacity to love despite the circumstances of unrequited love.

The lesson is not to ever lose oneself in waiting for love to manifest. Love just is and has already manifested. Love resides within. It is just a matter of which degree of love is present. If expected degrees of love is not reciprocated, it's no reflection on the individual who is ready. Love not the idea of love, but fall in love with the reality, and learn to govern self according to what is being presented. Stand in the power of one's own boundaries, and accept nothing less than what is truly affirmed. The lesson is for one to know that they are enough, and regardless of past mistakes, love is deserved by all, simply because our existence begins and ends with the lover of all souls. When love is willing to go beyond the recesses of darkened pain in others, the bond is immeasurably powerful. Live not on empty promises, and know that love should not be based on materialistic reality. It should be based on the authenticity of the individual in totality, flaws as well as laudable attributes. Love prevails the fiery flames of the past, accepts and guides one to their fullest potential.

Self-Check

What have your relationships taught you about you?

_____

_____

_____

_____

_____

_____

_____

In preparation for Emotional Exfoliation, jot down your beliefs or issues which act as a roadblock to you having a lasting relationship.

_____

_____

_____

_____

_____

_____

_____

8 unKonditional
FRIENDSHIP

Intentional deceit, a trick of the enemy, will cost you far more than honoring the value of the soul with openness and honesty, no matter how costly, even the price of the relationship.

i. Philia

Commonly referred to as brotherly love, Philia is love without romantic attraction and occurs between friends or family members. Intrinsically, it is a part of philautia, because it bathes in the same waters as self-love in that it is essentially "another you" or "another oneself." You share the same values and respect for each other as of course you too value self worth and respect of self. We share this kind of love with people who share in our opinions, attitudes, and beliefs. It is the variant of love that blossoms among platonic friends. So, the driver or catalyst to this type of love stems from the mind.

Throughout life, we will find ourselves in relationships, be it familial, romantic, professional, or friendly. Commonalities in the relationship are an extension of a dimension of personality within an individual. There is something everyone can learn from others. They can expose those unhealed parts of one's own personality. Some say relationships mirror back to a person what they refuse to acknowledge within themselves.

How is it even recognized in others if it is not present within oneself? That seems to be the consensus, but I have mixed emotions about it. Not every time is it about the darkness within one person that attracts someone else. It is the light within them we should place our focus. There is something that they do well that might be underdeveloped within our own trauma. That darkness has nothing to do with anyone else.

We don't base the attraction on darkness alone. There could be some truth to that, but we should base friendships on commonality and agreeability. Like souls attract to each other. Hopefully, people who find themselves in relationships can relate to each other in ways that may not seem possible to others. There should not be any conditions in the way genuine friendship exemplifies support and acceptance.

There is no hint of manipulation in the bond of friendship. The intent to control another person is not the basis of genuine friendship, let alone unconditional friendship. In unconditional friendships, friends support each other whether or not they agree with certain decisions, always refraining from judgment. It is not a general rule that friends must agree on every given thing, but there must always be respect and trust in everything.

Friends should be comfortably transparent, and we should respect their space and freedom to be who they are, authentically. There must be unwavering trust in that the individual is capable to decide according to what seems best for them and genuine respect for that person's final decision. That's not to say that dialogue, debate, suggestive alternatives, and vetting doesn't take place before that final decision is made. The iterative dialogue process which skips combative tones is a healthy exchange in a caring relationship.

An unconditional friend is there through any elected decision, be they good, bad, or indifferent. Unconditional friends do not cross that dictatorial combative boundary when interjecting their own opinions in an attempt to influence the life of the other person because their input is not derived from a selfish origin of manipulation. An unconditional caring friend will aide you in thinking through the alternatives of the matter while allowing you the space to choose and will walk the mile to support, come what may, no matter the final choice.

Unconditional friends respect their personal space and remain non-invasive but not necessarily dormant in regards to others' personal decisions. Although extreme, what non-invasive friend worth being a friend would allow you to jump off of a 200 foot cliff without a parachute, hang glider, tested bungee chord, rappel rope secured at the top, or the absence of a belay man without strongly cautioning you at the very least? Or what about a more common occurrence, drinking and driving or leaving a club drunk with a total stranger?

A friend's care, control and protection has its place, but the key point is that a healthy friendship has boundaries and the wisdom or discernment to know the coordinates of those survey stakes by which the boundary lines are drawn. What one wants most is loving acceptance, unconditional support and an "I got your back" mentality. Rejection by someone once considered a friend can be devastating, but it's an all too common occurrence. A person has every right to change their mind about a decision, and an unconditional friend supports the first, second and last decision because of mutual respect for the other person to live how they choose. This is not in support of a hands off relationship, rather one of ultimate acceptance. Unconditional friends will never intentionally compromise the trust and respect of the friendship. These types of friends are unconditionally loyal to each other based on an informal mutual contract, but that loyalty does not stem from one's dependence on or need for the other person. In the perfect relationship, there is no weighty concern for betrayal because an acceptable comfort level of trust in unconditional relationships is sufficiently evident. Please understand that extraneous things happen in any relationship that can potentially break a bond like a category 5 twister of 250 mph winds sending shards of wood into the depths of a brick wall. Nothing is perfect but the Creator, however, this is representative of the ideal friendship template. At it's best, no matter what, things revealed within the sanctuary of that relationship will remain between the two, never to be exposed even in bouts of anger.

Respect is gained when unconditional honesty is present in friendship. Even when one thinks or knows that their disclosure, disagreement, rebuke or relation threatening truth will hurt, and more than likely it will, the friend on the receiving end will appreciate or at least accept the honest truth. People in genuine relationships with each other deserve the truth whether one believes the other can handle it or not, even if it means the demise of the relationship, respectfully. Intentional deceit, a trick of the enemy, will cost you far more than honoring the value of the soul with openness and honesty, no matter how costly, even the price of the relationship.

Honesty sets you free from having to live a double life. As a rule of thumb, one should honor another's right to honesty, and, so, almost never rob another person's right to make a choice simply because of your fear that the nature of the revelation of your truth may invoke undesirable behavior or choice in that the recipient cannot handle the disclosure. Intentional non-disclosure is not the same vehicle as intentional deceit, but it is dishonest; some things are better left unsaid. Not everything in one's life is declared automatically up for discussion.

Privacy is to be respected at all costs. Relationships exist for a reason or a season. It is a blessing to have a friendship that lasts a lifetime, for it has lasting reason. Amicable relationships should not feel like a tug of war. Granted, "good days always" will not be status quo, but there should never be a time when struggle arises within the relationship without attempted resolution within that relationship.

Pettiness is undesirable and should not be left unaddressed as it may undermine the relationship and point to deeper concern, evidence of a misguided heart. Immaturity is somewhat different in that it may not stem from a coarse heart, but it too should be addressed through measures of correction and growth. If maturity is not the issue, then, it is simply an act of questionable character, in which case, it then mirrors pettiness. The riddle, "sticks and stones may break my bones, but words will never hurt me" is an absolute myth. Words indeed hurt like a forceful blow to the gut. They are a surgical scalpel that can slice through ligaments and tendons of confidence and trust with ease in any relationship. The intentional infliction of pain or uneasiness onto others is a direct reflection of the callous heart of the aggressor, and that is indicative of the pain and disease that resides within the perpetrator.

The human psyche can only pour out what was already within. Whatever inner struggles an individual deals with soon projects outward toward those whom they are in constant contact with or just the person they deem worthy of that kind of venom. The mask a person wears to deceive another's perception of them soon fades, simply because one cannot deviate from what is natural and normal for too long.

There is no way one can continually conceal the hateful spirits that infects their character. It soon shows up in how they treat others, usually through some triggered event. Judging someone based on what is heard or thought to be true speaks more about the individual making the judgment than it does about the individual being judged.

It is shameful how many people want to be treated and regarded with respect but are eager to offer the exact opposite at every opportunity. The basis of any unconditional relationship is being true and respectful to self by not allowing others to disrespect your moral ground and standards. Any kind of behavior that does not serve the Highest Good of all involved should be checked.

That faded reflection in the mirror indicated to me that I took better care of other people's feelings than I did my own. I had to learn to put my feelings and desires first while not being disrespectful to others, not in a selfish kind of way, but in a way to honor how I felt about things. I operated out of the fear of being called problematic by disregarding a lot of things, not challenging anything. I would not confront issues because my need to be liked and accepted took precedence over my need to be heard.

When I got to a place where I wanted to live true to myself, I had to start voicing how I felt. When I started voicing how I felt, my friendships started to wane, but I had to learn to accept the consequences without prejudice. I became unconditionally honest about what I felt with respect for what others felt as well. I had to realise that my feelings mattered too. While I may not be perfect, I deserve to surround myself with people who have genuine respect for the things that matter to me just the same as I respect what matters to them.

Despite any effort to appease certain relationships, somehow, one by one, they all fell apart. It is sad because I was now losing relationships that meant something to me. But I had to quickly learn to accept that despite my efforts to hold on to those relationships, I must unequivocally hold on to me first.

I CHOOSE ME! Along with being called evil and crazy and referred to as a terror, I have been called lonely, miserable and depressed by so many people I thought to be my friends. I would hide my desires for love because I didn't want to be referred to as lonely and miserable. It has been done so much until now it has become quite comical.

What baffles me is that while everything was amicable, within those same relationships, we were all having the same conversations of misery, but somehow now I am the one accused of stepping outside of that box they preferred to keep me in, voicing my opinion about what we all were feeling, and I become the lone sheep, the only one that's miserable, the outlier, the problem. What is it about people and their fear of being truthful about their feelings? It's the fear of the light that vulnerability shines highlighting what they mistake as weakness. I get it, it's twisted, and only a few know how to untwist and successfully drink the potion of the exposure of a vulnerable trait or state.

In unconditional friendships, mistakes are made without condemnation. In this life, nothing rests, everything is in motion, even inanimate objects. Everything is about energy, and when a person begins to vibrate on different levels, it is highly likely that some relationships will be lost. Changed energy in relationships results in growth in a different direction. Changed energy opens the way for new friendships that are in alignment with the evolved individual. I admit I may not have always been the best person or friend, but I was truthful about what I believed.

I was not the best manager of my emotions. I wore my heart on my sleeves and would blow up at any given moment the landmine of my emotions was stepped on. My emotions were like ticking time bombs waiting to be detonated. I am apologetic for my inability to manage those emotions properly, but I will never apologize for having them. It was certainly easy to push my buttons, and I would react without fail quite hastily.

Even with my flaws and all the mistakes I have made, nothing I have done has warranted me to have experienced some of the horrible treatment I have endured. When love is for real, it should never be a moment where the motive is to intentionally inflict pain. And when it does, that speaks to either the level of love or maturity of the individual. To be successful in relationships with other people, one must be successful in a relationship with themselves.

ii. Pragma

Pragma is a variant of love derived from the Greek to mean businesslike. This kind of love is pragmatic in nature meaning that it is practical. It is not born out of romantic love. It is a love of convenience. This kind of love is for those individuals who find themselves in relationships of convenience that are perceived to be rational.

Pragma is based on logic and reason, and its catalyst is etheric, astral, the collective unconscious or subconscious, the possible link between our finite mind and Infinite intelligence. From a romantic relationship perspective, any relationship that either started in or never experiences Eros love is possibly a variation of pragmatic relationships. People who engage in pragmatic relationships turn a blind eye to any kind of other real attraction. Pragma love is experienced by those individuals who come together for a common goal. Pragma relationships are built on mutual interest not to be confused with mutual love. They are mutually compromising and tolerable.

Commonalities in pragmatic relationships are the mutual interests that individuals in those relationships value. While pragmatic love is necessary for a variety of reasons, it's questionable that those individuals are fulfilled. These relationships are arranged for reasons other than veritable love.

Pragmatic relationships consists of people who choose to go through the motions and avoid emotions of substance. The fear of vulnerability is what pushes individuals into these types of relationships. Indeed, there is some degree of love or concern in these relationships, but it is difficult to affirm that this kind of love feeds the soul.

"These relationships more so feed the flesh. If, and only if, practical love is the soul's ultimate desire, then these relationships have a good chance of lasting. The practicality and realism of pragmatic love often contributes to the longevity of the relationship if common goals and values remain shared."[33]

The bigger question becomes, "What happens when the common interest or goal is reached or no longer relevant?" The relationship will more than likely end at that point. The relationship has the potential to become poisonous if a partner no longer sees the value in the common goal.

Of course, I have found myself in pragmatic relationships. Who hasn't? OK, maybe you haven't, but for me, the agreement was not financial in nature, but there were certainly benefits. I don't regret the experience of those situations. However, I do regret not having the courage to be vulnerable and ask for what I truly wanted in situations that really mattered. In some instances, I even lied to myself, telling myself that a relationship was not what I was looking for at the time, but the truth was that I was afraid to ask for anything more because I was afraid of being rejected. So, I allowed myself to remain in those situations that didn't serve the highest degree of what I desired. The fear of love not being returned crippled me from being true to myself. I accepted what was being offered because I was afraid. Fear stupefied me, in the sense that I would abandon myself to avoid the burden of unrequited love or affection. Because I could not find the courage to ask for what I needed, the whole situation was tainted with the fact that I settled.

I settled for orgasmic pleasure, which was fine, but I wanted more and was too afraid to express that desire. There were some good moments shared, but no purpose was served because it was less than that which I desired. It was what I will call "fauxlicity" to coin a term, not authentic felicity. The faded reflection once again revealed to me that I had lost several

---

[33] Wikipedia, https://en.wikipedia.org/wiki/Color_wheel_theory_of_love, The Color Wheel theory of love. 2020, accessed February 20, 2021

years wasting time in situations that I knew would never evolve into what I needed or desired.

I think spending time in those loveless relationships was a contributing factor in growing doubt within myself. However, in my growth, I had to accept that I could not place blame on anyone but myself because I allowed it. I cheated myself out of opportunities to find and have someone who would return love. How could I expect to be treated any better than I was treating myself? I had allowed time to pass in hopes that I could convince a hopeful that I was worthy of love, but to no avail. That day would never come. It was a slap in the face to hear that there was not even a thought of solidifying a relationship when time and opportunity presented itself, an eye opener to say the least. And in that moment, I gained the courage to let go.

I do understand the actions of others have equal influence and contribution to the vacancy of love in Hotel Pragma, but in this instance, it had everything to do with me in that I was allowing it in my life. I strap on full accountability for my part in those situations. Placing blame would not have done anything at all to resolve the situation. It was time I saw it for what it was and no longer walk down that path because it would lead to nothing but wasted time and empty dreams. It was time out for allowing myself to remain in loveless situations, because I deserved better. That was something I had to learn for myself though.

iii. Astorgos/Hate

Love and hate occupy opposing ends of a very complex spectrum. This spectrum is varied because of the degree of intensity of each emotion. The principle of polarity affirms that in life there is always balance, because everything is dual and has its pair opposites. They are identical in nature, but they differ in degree. That being the case, it is reasonable to believe that hatred can be unconditional just as love is unconditional. There are some who can be so consumed with hatred that it does not matter how much good is done, hatred is the only emotion to be expressed. When the heart of a person is filled with hatred, they tend to thrive on negativity which easily morphs into evil.

They celebrate opportunities to display disdain on any playing field. These individuals are quite clever at masquerading hate as love. If feelings of love can quickly turn into hate, then the degree of love is questionable. While there is a thin line between love and hate, it is not feasible to believe that one can readily transmute genuine love into any degree of genuine hate.

It seems to be trending in society that expressing tenderness for others is a thing of the past. Society is bent on not showing vulnerability because it is thought of as being "thirsty" or in other words desperate. It seems that public displays of any degree of hate, in the minds of many, equates to strength. Narcissism borders on a degree of hate. That kind of love is egotistical and pompous. It comes in the form of conceit and vanity. It is only interested in what is beneficial for self. This kind of love has little to no concern for others. It is selfish and prideful. It is rude and condescending. It owns no fault and only places blame. Recall that this is akin to amour popre, self-esteem. Talk about a thin line between love and hate — betcha never looked at self-esteem in the same light.

Self-adulation also rides on the rails of a gradient that crosses the line of healthy love and narcissism. Toot your own horn — just not too too loud, right? Well, I guess. Accountability is foreign to the narcissistic soul. The narcissistic soul is materialistic and will stop at nothing to soothe its own ego. People who love within the degree of hate allow malicious intention to govern their behavior. It is not a question of whether love and hate exist, it is to what degree a person chooses to render love/hate. Maybe it is not a question of choice but a question of capacity.

As simple as that concept may seem, people can only give love to the degree in which they have received love. But even that is not absolute because there are some that can give love in a positive way despite their experiences with insufficient or deceptive love. The polarity of the propensity of the individual determines the degree to which love and or hate is rendered.

Some may feel that love and hate is rare and that could possibly imply their doubt that true love and or hate exists. Neither love nor hate is rare. People just seem more inclined to openly express degrees of hate because we live in a world that mocks any show of love or vulnerability. So, to avoid looking weak or desperate, we hesitate when it comes to showing love. On the contrary, avoidance of public display of any degree of hate is less likely because it is more readily acceptable in the minds of many.

Self-Check

How have you altered what you believe about yourself based on someone else's inability to befriend you?

_____

_____

_____

_____

_____

_____

_____

What have you gotten the courage to face about yourself because of a friendship you were involved in? things you refuse to accept?

_____

_____

_____

_____

_____

_____

_____

9 unKonditional
FORGIVENESS

Hanging on to anger grounds you while grasping onto a compromised power line; it only damages the one who holds on to it.

i. The Law of Forgiveness

The law of forgiveness is about forgiving oneself first. There is no question about the ability to forgive others when one learns to forgive themselves first. A brush stroke at the art of forgiving oneself is found in the ability to convince the psyche that in every situation, whatever action was taken was the best action your mind could sanction in the heat of the moment. The bad decision was based on the immediate knowledge, feelings and/or emotions, or absence thereof, derailing the individual's decision making process or perhaps inducing a chemical imbalance at that time.

If poor decisions are made with all the information available, the ability to adjust and make a new decision is of most importance. In that situation, the key is accountability. Owning one's actions is the best way to facilitate a resolve if there was any breakdown in the relationship. Too often, accountability is the missing ingredient in the resolution, be it with self or others. Even when one needs to forgive themselves, they must first acknowledge and account for the mistake, intentional or not. We must learn to take the good with the bad and realise that there is always opportunity to atone even if it doesn't or can't effect an outcome of reversal which makes things right. There is no reason not to forgive when we understand that we and others are doing the best that we all can in every circumstance.

Forgiveness is a change in one's attitude. It is a shift in perspective toward others and circumstances. It is a decision to give up anger and replace it with acceptance. People make the choice to behave the best way they see fit, and because of free-will within the moral will of God, they have the freedom to make that morally acceptable choice. Acts of immorality are not sanctioned by God and are to be condemned by society. Forgiveness is the conscious decision to release anger and resentment.

Hanging on to anger grounds you while grasping onto a compromised power line; it only damages the one who holds on to it. Unconditional forgiveness should never emulate the shape of a question mark, given the destructive internal effects of harboring negative emotion. Holding on to negative energy has adverse effects on the body. This energy is very real and consists of untamed free radicals with unstable electrons causes cell destruction and causes internal chaos, damage to organs. Negative energy serves as a blocker to the flow of positive energy. Forgiveness ensures the flow of healthy internal energy and improves the quality of life, sparing the organs.

Decreased feelings of anger and anxiety minimizes stress when one can find the courage to soften their heart and release resentment. Though emotions are not tangible, they produce an incredibly powerful energy that can be felt by the body as research confirms that harboring negative emotion can damage cardiovascular, nervous, and immune systems. They have also shown that the practice of forgiveness improves physical health.[34]

[34] Terrell, Jon. 2012 – 2020. Help with grief, anger, fear, and other difficult emotions. https://emotional-healing.org/

Holding on to anger gives others more power than they deserve. If someone makes a choice to behave in ways that could prove destructive to the relationship, it is best to set oneself free from the weight of judgment and hostility. That is the time to decide whether the relationship is worth saving or time to let it go. It is not fair to self to subject you to abuse of any kind. Releasing ill emotion frees that individual from developing a resentful nature. Holding on to anger alters the internal nature of that person, and no one should allow the actions or behavior of others to alter them negatively.

The goal is to be steadfast. People will perform many tricks just to get a reaction. They thrive on that kind of pettiness, and when they know they can push your buttons, they will stop at nothing to antagonize, knocking you off your balance beam. The prudent thing for you is recognition and avoidance. Dismount, executing a perfect double somersault onto the mat; Stick, curtsy, and waltz right past the instigator.

Forgiveness is different from condoning, which is failing to condemn the action as though the action is acceptable and, therefore, not wrong nor in need of penitence and forgiveness. "Excusing is not holding the offender responsible for the action, forgetting is removing awareness of the offense from consciousness, and pardoning is granting forgiveness for an acknowledged offense by a representative of society, such as a judge, and reconciliation is the restoration of a relationship."[35]

Forgiveness is a process by which the offended overcomes unforgiving emotions, an unburdening of negative energy or emotion. It is a conscious and deliberate agreement one makes with themselves to release all feelings of resentment and or revenge toward other people for offensive acts that

---

[35] Mary Fairchild. (2019) What does the Bible say about Forgiveness...https://www.learnreligions.com/what-does-the-bible-say-about-forgive ness-701968

may have caused emotional discomfort. It is also a deliberate agreement one should make to release all feelings of shame and guilt toward themselves.

The use of the word "should" is pertinent here, because people do tend to leave themselves out of the forgiveness process. Another brush stroke at the art of forgiving oneself is found in the ability to realise and understand that in every situation whatever decision not charged with negative intent was the best decision derived in that moment. The real complication becomes evident when mal intent is involved. Then, the aforementioned brushstroke in convincing the psyche becomes applicable.

The process of forgiveness happens in phases and often does not happen overnight. The first phase of the forgiveness process is for one to acknowledge the true reasons the anger exists. The key to forgiveness is acknowledgment. One, first, must find the courage to admit that they hurt someone or have been hurt themselves, instead of lashing out in mindless anger.

Forgiveness cannot be anticipated without confessions of some sort. This can be difficult living in a society that readily condemns someone for showing any kind of vulnerability. Either we have conditioned ourselves or we have been conditioned to believe that showing real emotion is a sign of weakness, being soft. It seems easier or perhaps more powerful to project feelings of rage rather than feelings of discomfort.

In many instances there are some who work overtime to prove how impervious they are to a thing, but in actuality, the need to express that one is unbothered is a true give away that they are in fact bothered. Don't get it twisted, there is power in vulnerability in the sense that forgiveness is enriched with power.

Ultimately, forgiveness is about oneself more than it is about other people. Just as everything else starts with self, so does forgiveness. It becomes easier to forgive others when one first learns to forgive themselves.

Forgiving oneself can be difficult to a degree. When things happen and the wrong decision is made or the wrong action is taken, sometimes a person can get so focused on trying to figure out ways they could have done better or made a better decision that they overlook the necessity of forgiving themselves. One must learn to accept that the best decision was made, excepting mal intent, based on the level of understanding at that time, then agree to make a better decision when levels of understanding have elevated.

It is counterproductive to go through life in constant meditation on mistakes of the past. It is not wise for one to punish themselves for things that were unknown at the time a decision was made. The best course of action is to learn to manage the decision that was made.

Managing a decision simply means to find the best course of action from the new point of reference. It is sensible to modify a new perspective and govern oneself accordingly. Harboring feelings of embarrassment for bad judgment is maleficent more for oneself than it is for others. Peace of oneself is compromised when lingering too long on what could have or should have been. That is time and attention wasted and focused on the wrong direction. It is not fair to hold self accountable for information that was not known in certain situations. Life unfolds exactly as it is supposed to, and it is prudent of you to trust that notion. It is not healthy or beneficial to go through life beating oneself up for self made poor decisions. The faded reflection in the mirror had to get in my face with this one. I am always harder on myself than I am with others.

Internalizing the embarrassment of bad decisions is certainly a pattern that we must change. It profits nothing, secretly beating up oneself for mistakes. We are human, therefore flawed. There should not be any pressure to be anything other than an individual doing and being the best version of flawed self.

The Law of Forgiveness states that one cannot be forgiven until they forgive others. If negative thoughts of anger, judgment and hatred are harbored against others, one will not find any peace within themselves because those feelings that are being harbored are also felt by the individual. The turmoil of negative emotions is bound to have some effect on other emotions felt by the individual. Negative emotion does not just go away. They grow and then manifest in other ways. Emotional freedom is the release or unburdening of unforgiving thoughts and feelings. One cannot fully expect to be forgiven if they are not willing to forgive.

The nature of forgiveness does not have to be perfect, but the willingness to try is of great worth. Forgiveness takes place in one of two ways, decisional or emotional. Decisional forgiveness is an intention to eliminate negative behavior associated with revenge while trying to restore interaction so long as the threat of future harm no longer exists. Emotional forgiveness replaces negative or unforgiving emotions with positive ones. The effort is made to replace negative emotions like anger and resentment with understanding emotions like empathy and compassion. Faux forgiveness decides to forgive while harboring a grudge, which is not true forgiveness. It is easy to decide to forgive transgression, but unconditional forgiveness is accompanied with the release of negative emotion as well.

As followers of any faith, believers are encouraged to forgive. In doing so, we should forgive as God has commanded.

a. Judaism

In Judaism, it is forbidden to be stubborn and not allow yourself to be appeased. On the contrary, one should be easily pacified and find it difficult to become angry. When asked by an offender for forgiveness, one should forgive with a sincere mind and a willing spirit. (Mishneh Torah, Teshuvah 2:10) Teshuvah is another word for repentance. The process of repentance is transpired in three distinct phases: confession, regret, and vow. If an individual causes harm but makes a sincere and honest effort to apologize, the person wronged is encouraged to forgive, but not required. In Judaism, a person cannot obtain forgiveness from God for wrongs they have committed against other people. One must go to those who have been harmed to be entitled forgiveness.

b. Christianity

Forgiving others affords God's forgiveness.

Matthew 6:14 "For if you forgive men, when they sin against you, your heavenly father will also forgive you." (KJV)

The central idea of forgiveness in Christianity is that God will do unto a person the way he has done unto others. If a person seeks the forgiveness of God, he or she must first be ready and able to forgive others. In response to Peter's question of incidence of forgiveness of an offending brother, Christ commanded in the book of Matthew 18:22 to forgive others seventy times seven times. Clearly, Jesus' point was that the Father forgives us of all our transgressions against Him, and that includes others. The Lord, then, is infinitely willing and able to forgive. So if we model after Him, we should not keep count of how many times we forgive. Jesus creates a link to the Father in that the Father "forgets" our transgressions and iniquity if we should be penitent and believe. In what I'm about to discuss and encourage walks in this light, but I even in my boldness, I am not so naive to think that human beings can forget offenses against us. But when we worship the Lord, we must worship in Spirit and in Truth. It is in this vein that I make my argument. In Spirit, we should always be willing to forgive as well as forget in Spirit. In no way am I indicating that we should be on and stay on a path of stupid. So, it is in this vain that I discuss the concept of healthiness through unconditional forgiveness and "forgetting" transgression against us.

1 John 1:9 "If we confess our sins, he is faithful and just to forgive us our sins and to cleanse us from all unrighteousness" (KJV) Unconditional forgiveness is similar in context to divine forgiveness.

c. Islam

Teaches that Allah is the original source of all forgiveness. It is considered a virtue to seek Allah's forgiveness with repentance. Because Allah values forgiveness, it is recommended for believers to forgive. Islam allows revenge to the extent harm was done but forgiveness is encouraged.

"The recompense for an injury is an injury equal thereto (in degree): but if a person forgives and makes reconciliation, his reward is due from Allah: for (Allah) loveth not those who do wrong." Quran 42:40

ii. Conditions of Forgiving

There should not be any conditions on one's capacity to forgive when their own peace of mind is in jeopardy. There is nothing that should prolong obstruction to a person's peaceful being, especially if it means letting go of emotions that are the result of an incident where one or both individuals refuse to address the problem directly. On the flip side, the refusal to address a problem is not always indicative of long drawn out grievances.

Sometimes relationships can be so poisonous that someone has reached the end of the line and no longer wishes to engage. That does not necessarily mean that unforgiveness is the final option; it could be that the individual is done attempting to salvage an expired relationship, and the best option would be to permanently part ways. In that instance its assumed that some degree of forgiveness has taken place and the issue is permanently settled in the individual's mind and heart. We have heard numerous times before that forgiveness is not for the other person. It is true, indeed, that forgiveness is for the individual.

In most cases, a person must be willing to forgive without having received an apology. Forgiveness takes place whether the offender deserves it or not. Also, it is necessary whether or not an apology is offered. There are strong arguments against holding on to pain and hurt feelings. It seems to take more energy to hold on to wounded emotions of the past than it does to release them and move on. The art of forgiveness says that one has the capacity to allow themselves to feel their emotions and then allow them to flow freely through.

The problem is not in feeling the pain — the problem comes when one holds on to pain, thus becoming stagnant in the battered emotions of the offense. It is not mentally or emotionally healthy to live life looking through bruised lenses. The soul's intent is not to operate from a place of pain and suffering. The lesson is to learn how to live from a state of grace.

Anger, hurt, and pain are all real and valid emotions, and it is meaningful for an individual to allow themselves permission to feel those feelings. Unconditional Forgiveness is not an automatic negation of the existence of an offense, nor does it excuse bad behavior. It does not even mean that the feelings of the offended are minimized or denied.

Because people have experienced numerous emotionally traumatic events, it is quite possible that they have not effectively dealt with angry or hurt feelings from other emotionally traumatic experiences. A person could have been triggered because of those unresolved experiences, and they do not realise they are upset about something completely different than what is happening real-time.

So, it is necessary that the offended gain clarity about the real reason they have become angry. Once this is achieved, they must give themselves permission to feel that anger or disappointment. Society has conditioned people to believe that feeling their emotions are a sign of weakness, and that is just not the case.

The allowance of oneself to feel their emotions is a sign of strength and maturity. As a person allows those feelings to exist within them, little by little those feelings begin to lessen. In life, things and or situations hurt us, and to heal, we must perform the 3R's, Release, Restore, Reshape.

Release the negative energy, Restore that wounded part of us and then Reshape our thoughts thus changing the outcome in the future. Not finding the courage to release the trauma of the experience will only taint the new experience.

People tend to bleed on other people in the exact place that they are bleeding themselves. The individual who suffers great pain is the individual who becomes capable of rendering great pain, but the worst victim is the one who actually makes a choice to inflict another in likeness.

"I can forgive, but I cannot forget," is an adage that most are accustomed to saying in the process of forgiving someone. Seems that this condition for forgiving is a nullifying and moot point. The chances of someone forgetting that a traumatic or hurtful experience took place are slim to none. So that statement has not much added value. There are some things like being severely and intentionally wronged that a person will not naturally forget. If such an offense transpired, ideally the victim should allow time for the diffusion of negative or vengeful emotions and then speak directly to the offender on the condition of a nonviolent offense and that no danger exists.

The problem with most adults is that they tend not to go directly to the person they are at odds with to address the issue(s). They will go to "everyone else." So, it is understandable to say that forgetting something is not likely, but to say, "I can forgive, but I cannot forget," is seemingly an oxymoron. To adamantly announce that the absence of forgetting is a condition attached to forgiving appears to be conditional for the purpose of holding on to the offense. True, we will not forget, but to say I will not forget, in a sense, colors the forgiveness disingenuous. If one decides to forgive another, why is there a need for a condition on forgiving; why mention the non-forgetting piece? It hides in plain sight the opportunity to use the offense at any given moment to manipulate an unattractive behavior in the other person.

Making the announcement of not forgetting harnesses the negative energy of the offense. Releasing the negative emotions associated with the offense is the premise of forgiveness, not whether one remembers or forgets. The effort should be placed on the conversation and amicable resolve of the issue, crediting the act of forgiveness to the wellness and emotional benefit to the harmed. Be convinced that you actually engaged in meaningful resolute conversation including contingency if appropriate, but otherwise unconditional. Spuriously, according to George Bernard Shaw, "The single biggest mistake in communication is the illusion that it took place." We have lost the ability to connect through vulnerability, the lens of intimacy in relationships.[36] Effective communication suffers greatly today.

Adults have lost the ability or desire to talk to each other and now with the conditioning of social media, as aforementioned, adults have effectively learned how to talk at each other and not to each other, replacing the art of conversation with subliminal posts and the usage of emoji and emoticon memes to mimic what they truly feel. To add insult to injury, the disclaimer, "this is not about me, it's just something that I can relate to," is illusory and diluting in and of itself.

Sometimes we hold on to unforgiveness because we are afraid of being hurt again, but life is about taking chances and the biggest chance is to relieve oneself of wounded emotions and trust that there is peace on the

---

[36] Shaw, George Bernard, https://quoteinvestigator.com/2014/08/31/illusion/

other side of the pain. Excessive meditation on the things that have not gone the way initially intended breeds more of the same. What we resist will persist.

The things a person meditates on the most is what is bound to manifest in their life and behavior. Meditation is not always about sitting in a yogic position uttering a chant. Meditation is anything that one places significant focus on. Unforgiveness is reactive instead of proactive. It takes more effort to hold on to bitterness than it does to let go and regain inner peace.

Forgiveness is not conditional. Conditional forgiveness says that there must be behavior or an act before pardon is given. Most times forgiveness comes easier upon acknowledgment of the offense. Life is hard enough, so there is no need to add to the strain by harboring ill-emotion toward someone who likely is unaware or unconcerned about bruised emotions.

If one is unwilling to directly address the person in question, then there is no point at all in holding on to the anger. It is possible that a person holds on to the anger because they want to use that anger and direct it back to the person who caused them pain in future situations. That kind of behavior is immature, heinous, and speaks directly to the character of the individual. It says more about their flawed level of integrity than it does about the intended target for harm.

What really happens is that anger gets held for an uncertain amount of time and more than likely gets displaced, and the aggression that was meant for a specific person is directed at someone else over something that didn't deserve that level of intensity. That happens because as spirited beings, it was never the intention of the Creator for us to harbor ill emotions. Not to discount anger at all, anger is indeed a valid emotion and should be expressed in the proper way to the appropriate degree.

Ephesians 4:26 "In your anger, sin not." (KJV).

Anger is not a sinful emotion. It is indeed as valid as any other emotion. One must learn to manage it appropriately. There is a lesson in any offense. After the initial shock of being betrayed or lied to has come and gone, the person who is courageous enough to look back at the faded reflection in the mirror can begin to search for breakdowns in their own behavior that contributed to or allowed the offense to occur. When I looked back in the mirror, I was able to see where my behavior sent the message that it was okay to misuse, mistreat or even abandon me.

And pay close attention to how I enumerate the behavior:

1) Misuse — 2) Mistreat — and even 3) Abandonment!!!

One and two are considered abuse, and yet I consider leaving the relationship to be more harsh than misuse and maltreatment. In my world, abandonment trumps abuse. How many more of you feel this way? I want to be clear that this is not normal, and neither is the concept of abandonment unless you're in a marital relationship, and then there are legal ramifications for abandonment.

Abandon defined is:

to leave and never return to (someone who needs protection or help)

to leave and never return to (something, not someone, may be a relationship)

to leave (a place) because of danger

Abandon is synonymous with desert or forsake meaning to leave without intending to return. Abandon suggests that the thing or person left may be helpless without protection such as an abandoned child of any age, a cripple such as a paraplegic, or an elderly person in serious decline.

So, let's be clear. We are not helpless abandoned children, newborn or otherwise. I get that, but yet my psyche was completely dependent on Eros, love, to a fault. I would condone the abuse if it meant that I wasn't left without a relationship, and in this manner, I was completely helpless, crippled and psychologically and emotionally dependent. Is this you?

Are you willing to stay in an abusive relationship to save yourself from being alone? When someone chooses to leave or abandon the relationship, they have also abandoned the abuse. Then how is this undesirable to you? I've learned that this is indeed tough when you do not want to be alone, but I recognize that if you do not stand for something, you will fall. And you will fall hard for anything unworthy of your time. This type of abandonment, we must realise, is actually a good thing. I implore you to realise that we must be advocates of such abandonment because we couldn't help ourselves, and the actuator of the parting of ways in such a relationship empowers us to stand and not fall for just anything.

That was the perfect opportunity for me to assess how I truly was showing up in my relationships. Perhaps my boundaries were too weak, non-existent even. If there is no consequence to wrong action or behavior, then it is true that I was sending the message to others that it was okay to behave badly.

So, the lesson I had to learn was to become more conscious of the messages that I was sending to those I was in relationship with. The faded reflection in my mirror also gave me the courage to stand boldly in the truth of how I feel. It has made me realise that my feelings matter. I have come to govern my life and my standards by changing the reflection that is staring back at me.

If I wanted righteousness from others, it meant I had to operate in righteousness myself or at least do my best anyway. Living in the freedom to amicably express what I was feeling was liberating. Speaking the truth of my feelings has shown me the truth of those with whom I was in a relationship: those who were egotistical and interested in what they could gain who had no respect for what was being expressed, and those who respected my feelings and gave me the space to express them.

I soon learned that I didn't have to chase people down to explain myself, and I made the decision not to do that any longer. Somewhere amid all the implications of my being evil or uncooperative, I adopted the thought that I needed to always explain myself and prove my good intentions. That faded reflection showed me that that was something I desperately needed to unlearn. I need not continue explaining myself to anyone who is committed to seeing me as undesirable. I had to accept that that is the way those individuals chose to see me, and no matter what I did, this is what they believed about me. There was no point in trying to change made-up minds about who I was and currently choose to be.

If there were some who refused to see exactly who I was and aspired to be, then that was their issue, not mine. It became too exhausting, walking on eggshells to ensure that I would remain in the good graces of everyone. An honest explanation was readily available for anyone who would address me directly and in mature fashion. Otherwise, it was my choice to let people believe whatever they chose.

There were times when I hid my truth for fear of not being liked or judged. I would find myself modifying my behavior to make other people feel comfortable in my presence. Why did I have to change to make them comfortable when they didn't change to make me comfortable? I was just as uncomfortable around them as they were around me. I learned to stand in the truth of who I was. My personality is big, true enough, but just because I had a fluid personality didn't make it acceptable for other people to try and minimize me because of their own insecurities. Genuine people don't have to dim the light in other people for their own light to shine.

I just came into agreement with myself, I discontinued overextending myself to prove anything to the likes of anyone who never took the opportunity to know and understand me for themselves. The problem is that most people tend to hold on and become so entangled in the "shoulda, woulda, coulda" that they go blind to any chances of facilitating a resolve within themselves.

There is peace on the other side of tragedy. It is senseless to live life full of regret for decisions that were made with the best intention. Even if the intention were not favorable, the best course of action would be to account for the wrong-doing and make amends. Signs of growth are indicative of the ability to admit bad behavior and follow it up with sincere apology.

Mistakes in judgment deserve no condemnation. Studies show that those individuals who readily forgive are significantly happier and healthier than those individuals who don't forgive. Forgiveness is believed to improve one's physical health. Thoughts of forgiveness lead to better functioning of a person's cardiovascular and nervous system.[37]

It has been said that those who have acquired the ability to forgive are less angry or hurt and have healthy optimism for the future. Whatever forgiveness is expected or desired from God should undoubtedly be bestowed upon others. It may be quite difficult because the human psyche does not easily let go of things, but the goal here is to strive to forgive as the Creator does.

I choose to set myself free from the weight of my own trauma. I forgive myself first for beating myself up for not knowing what to do to save her. I forgive myself for the trauma I inflicted upon myself because of my own toxic way of thinking and believing. I want to experience total healing, free of pain. My inner demons kept me believing that I was not good enough as

---

[37] Van Oyen, C. Witvilet. T.E Ludwig and KL Vander Lann, Granting Forgiveness, or harboring Grudges: Implications for emotions, Physiology and Health, Psychological Science no. 12 (2001): 117-23.

they show up in my insecurities, and I wrestle with them to maintain my sanity.

When I think about my thirteen year old self, all I can see is her sitting in a corner with her knees bent and her head hung, immersed in her own sadness and not knowing how to process that emotion properly. She tucked herself in that corner because blocking people out was her way of protecting her from pain. That is how I have seen young self.

Forgiving oneself and others is a perfect segue into an oasis of complete Healing power because it requires letting go, freeing up, and thereby exfoliating destructive emotions which enhances the navigability of travel through trauma.

Self-Check

What have you not forgiven yourself for?

_____

_____

_____

_____

_____

_____

Are you in need of forgiveness for anything that you've done to anyone?

_____

_____

_____

_____

_____

_____

10 unKonditional
HEALING OASIS

Exfoliating is like the slogan for milk, "it does the body good," but emotional exfoliation, "It does the mind even better," so that both your skin and emotions are healthy, radiant, silky smooth, balanced, vibrant, and felicitous.

Drowning in an abyss of guilty emotion is as a whirlpool funneling and spiraling you downward, opposing freedom of surfacing and forward movement. Too much time spent on things that are no longer in the span of one's control is destructive. True, sometimes it may be hard to let things go, but the desire for mental and emotional freedom should fuel the flame and spark a motivated effort to move through the minefield of pain.

There is a permanent wound in my heart, but I choose not to let it keep me in bondage because of my own pain. I am free in my heart. I am free in my spirit. I am free because I say so. The dark knight of the soul had the dubious honor of revealing through my traumatic experience that I was alone and unprotected in the world. I don't want to live life from a hurt place. So, I must rid myself of all emotional toxicity, and now I know that I can accomplish that through emotional exfoliation.

Emotional Exfoliation

I define Emotional Exfoliation as the process of removing unhealthy emotions from the abyss of the soul, which includes the psyche, using conventional and unconventional methods to surface and exterminate one's innermost dark matter as a release of traumatic stress. Bon voyage!

So, you've weathered many storms in your lifetime, young or older. You've battled and sustained bruises. You've survived, albeit barely, perhaps; nevertheless, you are survivor material. That's highly commendable, but don't get too relaxed. You've never encountered warfare like this before. You're in the desert weathering blistering heat. The sand is so hot, transforming into glass beneath the soles of your blistered feet. You may as well be walking through a fire pit on a bed of hot rocks without your training shoes. A windstorm is coming inevitably and spontaneously. You have nowhere to hide. It's inescapable, given your current mindset. You're not just in a pressure cooker, but a countertop convection oven where the 450° wind current encircles you at 5200 rpm, the heat vectors frying your skin to a crisp, peeling it away to your inner flesh, exposing your inner creation down and done to the bone. There is one consolation; You will be perfectly cooked crispy bacon as all the grease is collected by the hot sand swirling around you. With all your pent up emotions, that's where you are today and where you're headed in the not so distant future — maybe not crispy bacon, but a perfectly roasted turkey or tender hen isn't far off. And as the intensity of heat increases, you experience mercy, a mirage of palm trees and a fresh water oasis, Lake Coeur d'Alene just beyond the grid of heat waves.

Considering that you are accountable for holding these emotions way too close to the breast for far too long, it's time for you to get your mind right. Focus and beam yourself up and out of this crisis into the center of the mirage flickering before your weary eyes where you envisage at the nucleus of Spa Oasis @ The Coeur d'Alene, a lavish therapeutic spa to sooth your wounds. Every part of you would thank you for treating yourself to one of the most prestigious spas on the planet with the breathtaking Coeur d'Alene Lake and snow capped mountains as the backdrop, a stark contrast to the desert you've been trekking nearly all your life. The cerulean hue of the lake is a non-faded mirror reflection of the azure sky and things are looking up for you. Sky juice races downward like Victoria Waterfalls, a South African multi-waterfall complex mixing with ancient glacial waters to cool the sizzle of your skin for much needed relief. Exfoliation begins. First class therapy at its finest, you'll find this far more soothing than two hours with your therapist.

Your body is a temple, and it deserves to have you treat it with such love and care that it wants to love you back — XXOO. When you inhale and tune up your body with spa-like relaxation including deep tissue massages, facial and body exfoliation removing many of the 300 million dead cells of skin, hot therapeutic rocks aligning your spine for sheer tranquility as it calms your nervous system, and 100 gallons of water from 19 jets reshaping your body every minute from every direction alternating from cold to hot, your mind finds it very convincing to exhale, relax, and make emotional strife a distant memory. You are spoiled with exotic flowers and incense, a full body emollient bath of exotic rubs, a Korean scrub, the best exfoliants that remove rough texture, uncovering smooth gold, glimmering of rejuvenation. All this topped off with middle eastern oils and herbs head to toe.

But the reason it takes convincing is due to blockades, barriers. Emotional blocks are the barriers set up by our mind as a natural defense system. Likewise, our bodies have a natural barrier system. And where does that come from? Design by Creation, Inc., of course. Our physical bodies were designed with a barrier of protection as well, the surface layer, our skin, which by the way is our body's largest organ protecting most of our internal organs and the ultra complex biological system. Take away this barrier, and lack of vulnerability soon dissipates along with our bodies. Yeah — poof — no magic required. Just as setting boundaries in relationships is important, so are the human defense mechanisms of barriers. But barriers require management and maintenance as we will see.

As discussed earlier, our Cell factories are 100% utilisation production facilities 24/7 with unmatched yield by any production facility on planet earth. These factories have a 100% utilisation rate for a lifetime with unchartered efficiency rates and at a breakneck replenishment pace. The Skin Cells Factory manufactures two primary products, Keratinocytes, responsible for 90% of the composition of our skin and melanocytes which determine skin color. This organ, skin, produces a by-product called squames or scales. Of the 50 to 70 billion cells that die per day per person, nearly 60 million are skin cells, the desquamation process. Notice the frailty of our bodies as we age significantly, and you may infer that the factories age with us, eventually slowing production and ultimately shutdown when our heart, the central power unit, shuts down.

"Our bodies contain an estimated 19 million skin cells for every inch of your body and 300 million skin cells total." [38]

The Korean body scrub is a very detailed and effective treatment which exfoliates every inch of the body, and you can see the benefit of such a thorough treatment just by looking at the discoloration of the fabric points of contact with your skin such as necklines, wrists, arms, armpits, thighs etc. Believe me, we need the maintenance.

We lose anywhere from 30,000 to 40,000 skin cells a minute. In 24 hours, we lose around 56 million dead skin cells. [And guess what? Death stinks — I know, right?] One person's contribution to the stench of the

---

[38] Physical and Emotional Exfoliation for Summer, By Lisa Stewart, Solia Spa and Peri Skin Care,
Skin Inc.,
https://www.skininc.com/treatments/body/Physical-and-Emotional-Exfoliation-for-Summer571139081.html

atmosphere creates a nice share of the dust we breathe daily, and this dust can weigh up to around nine pounds in one year according to Lisa Stewart, esthetician and founder of Solia Spa and Peri Skin Care. She cites that dead skin cells contribute approximately one billion tons of dust in the earth's atmosphere. The squames from the skin of the human body contain keratin (structural proteins) that degrade by keratinase, enzymes produced by some bacteria. The released protein-based fuel source is then consumed by bacteria and broken down into ammonium. With limited amounts of carbon available in the environment, it can lead to excessive amounts of ammonium being emitted into the air and having a urine-like smell. There are also other microbial nutrients from skin squames that are consumed by these bacteria to emit a body odor smell. Display footnote number: 1, 2"[39]

Everything comes with risk as we elaborated in risk assessment and management, and going to a spa and stripping down butt-naked being atop treatment tables completely places one in a vulnerable but yet satisfying position. But not only that, if we overdo it, the skin becomes vulnerable with increased sensitivity to the harshness of UV rays and the heat of the sun as well as the chemical exfoliants themselves. Skin exfoliation is a wonderful treat, facial and full body, recommended by the experts at least once per month, but not much more because it weakens the skin by stripping down too deep to layers rendering unhealthy exposure. Well, opening up about your trauma places you in as vulnerable a position as the physical, but it is a necessary evil for folks suffering from Post Traumatic Stress Disorder (PTSD). We not only need to exfoliate dead skin, but we

---

[39] Dead cell references

1. http://biofuelsdigest.com/nuudigest/2018/01/31/oh-smell-that-smell- deadsk-in-cells-responsible-for-office-stench/

2. www.newsweek.com/bacteria-feast-dead-human-skin-live-inside- airconditioners-and-make-our-rooms-796803

must also exfoliate smelly, buried, toxic emotions. So, we term that emotional exfoliation.

Emotional Exfoliation is not without vulnerability or risk, hence emotional barriers, but it can be managed when done properly. In writing this book, I'm doing just that, and it feels incredibly soothing — and yes, I do feel vulnerable with all this exposure, but it's worth it as I can already sense results on a macro scale. It's like dead cells, scarred emotions stink up the atmosphere of my existence, tainting my thoughts, my response in relationships, my self esteem, the health and wealth of my mind, my psyche, and my physical well-being. I mean, you've heard motivational speakers, pastors, bishops, coaches and the like idiomatically exclaim, "Get rid of your stinkin' thinkin'!" Well now you know it's origin, and it can be translated in the literal sense.

Viewing trauma, many confuse drama with trauma. There are those who believe that they are experiencing trauma in that drama invades their emotions. Although I'm not a licensed practitioner, I am certainly a bonafied case of trauma and, therefore, affected patient of the dangers of PTSD due to firsthand experience, unfortunately. I can tell you that trauma and drama are no more interchangeable than expand and expound, affect and effect. In all three cases, the key element is point of reference. While both expand and expound share the terms elaborate and detail, point of reference for expand is the already stated or preexistence of the thought or topic while expound comes at the same from a fresh or newly stated perspective. Influence is relative to both effect and affect, however effect (the what) is the resulting action or the actual influence, and affect (the how) is the cause or influence or effect on something or someone. In the case of drama and trauma, drama evokes a reaction in us from a sudden or unexpected occurrence, but it does not cause physical harm or deep rooted nerve or psychological damage and longterm suffering ever, while trauma inflicts injurious harm and lasting pain physically and/or emotionally. From the pragmatist's perspective, one should follow the logical professional route to unseed and surface the root cause of trauma.

a. Scribe and Strike Methodology

But other methods are helpful, including Scribe and Strike Methodology which we practised earlier, and we will implement or effect as an iterative process in our lives and once more momentarily. Expose your trauma through scripting the event and your entrapped feelings, coaching emergence and ultimately it's release, then strike through your penned experience(s). Perform this rite as often as required to exhume the buried toxic matter, casketing it in a journal, a diary, a notepad, an I-pad or similar device such as a notebook or laptop, and strike through every single word, then write that you declare those emotions dead, gone, exfoliated. The immediate next step is to think of positive words to describe you and your heart's desires, making a strong claim that you can have the best of this life, that it is within your reach and in your future. But you could start with simply acknowledging your own beauty, no matter the category.

Acknowledge self-love. I know that I love me some me! I am awesome in my own unique way. Clean out the mental and emotional closet, and stock it with fresh, bright thoughts, feelings, and desires riding a wave of high frequencies that vibrate out into the cosmos on an elliptical path that booms and boomerangs right back to you, shaping your future with the clay of authentic felicity, love, confidence and abundance.

This method of emotional exfoliation is an iterative process just as dead cell exfoliation is, and as an expert concerning being on the front line of PTSD, I personally do this as oft as possible without seeming to obsess over the graphic matter, which could be equally damaging. If your trauma tracks anything similar to the pattern of my own, you will have emotional lapses and will need to scribe and strike again. With each exercise, you will get stronger and more efficient at managing your emotional trauma through self spa treatment.

Experience on aisle 7, the hygiene section at the local supermart, stocked with several products specifically to exfoliate skin whether through scrubs, rubs, soaps, chemicals, or specialized mechanical devices, teaches us that exfoliating is a multi-billion dollar industry and at least a trillion cells cleansing industry. Exfoliating is like the slogan for milk, "it does the body good," but emotional exfoliation, "It does the mind even better" so that both your skin and emotions are healthy, radiant, silky smooth, balanced, vibrant, and felicitous.

The experts may suggest facial and body exfoliating treatment at least once a month, but If we look beyond the surface of facials and body and focus on what the soul needs from head to toe, emotional exfoliation should be done as often as daily, no less than weekly. You're nurturing the soul and that makes God your source and truly the only expert that matters. Give in to His guidance as you are in prayer and in connect with Him spirit to Spirit, daily.

Emotional exfoliation goes one step further to exempt the mind from thinking negative thoughts, to rid your heart of negative energy and negative frequencies.

Matt 6:21 states "For where your treasure is, there your heart will

be also." (NKJV)

Matthew 12:34 And so "For out of the abundance of the heart, the mouth speaks." (NKJV)

Water is alive and apparently sensitive, but not only that, it too has memory, but speak to it a certain way, and guess what? — Straight Jackettttt!!!!!! I kid, I kid. True, water is alive, but no, it is not proven that water is sensitive in the sense of feelings nor has "water memory" been confirmed beyond questionable findings by Jacques Benveniste in 1988 as differing results show in controlled research by third party agencies through 2014. In fact, Peter Fisher, the editor of Homeopathy, acknowledged that Benveniste's original method does not yield reproducible results and declared " ... the memory of water is a bad memory: it casts a long shadow over homeopathy and is just about all that many scientists recall about the scientific investigation of homeopathy, equating it with poor or even fraudulent science."[40] In a controlled setting, no team has been able to replicate his study in reference to memory. Seems sadly a bit traumatic in and of itself for homeopathy. But plants is a different story. According to a study conducted by the Royal Horticultural Society over the course of a month, plants can and do hear the human voice as well as adapt and react, albeit not in the same way that humans do. The plants that were read to daily by males and females grew more than those lacking human dictation. Further, those plants which were spoken to by females grew an inch more than those read to by males. Plants begin to hear at 70 decibels which just so happens to coincide with the average frequency of the human voice according to Research by South Korea's National Institute of Agricultural Biotechnology. Research conducted by Evolutionary Biologist, Monica Gagliano, also proved that pea seedlings responded to other sounds of their environment, such as running water — they tended to grow towards an enclosed tube of running water closer to one set of plants versus the other only having dry soil in their immediate vicinity. Why is this? Well, words

---

[40] ∧ a b J. Maddox; J. Randi; W. W. Stewart (28 July 1988). ""High-dilution" experiments a delusion". Nature. 334 (6180): 287–290. Bibcode:1988Natur.334..287M. doi:10.1038/334287a0. PMID 2455869.

∧ J. Benveniste (28 July 1988). "Dr Jacques Benveniste replies" (PDF). Nature. 334 (6180): 291. Bibcode:1988Natur.334..291B. doi:10.1038/334291a0. Archived from the original on 18 October 2009.

∧ Maddox, J., Randwi, J. & Stewart, W. "High-dilution" experiments a delusion. Nature 334, 287–290 (1988). https://doi.org/10.1038/334287a0

and sound are powerful! They have vibrational frequencies according to the Law of Attraction.

Plants are not as emotionally complex as humans, so you can't hurt their feelings even though the louder and the more you speak to them, or the more music you play around them, the more they respond. But because of the vibrational frequencies generated when we speak, they acknowledge whether we're giving off good, bad, or stoic vibes. To be clear, sound, any sound within their audible or vibrational range of frequency, is all they perceive.

For us, positive thoughts accompanied by positive posture vibrate out at higher frequencies. The more one postures positively and focuses on uplifting things, the more they will attract positive outcomes, maybe even windfalls. The same applies for those which vibrate out lower energy frequencies, they will attract back to them that which they vibrate out, negativity. Your vocabulary is far more powerful than you realise, and your thoughts are forever in sesh and, so, are even more powerful. Your tongue, though, is a double edged sword.

Therefore, if negative thoughts fill your temple abundantly as treasure, your tongue will utter the same, soliciting negative deeds to be drawn to you. But if your treasure chest is filled with positive thoughts, then your life will flourish with positivity in return. ***In the moment that you become a champion of you, validation of who you are is certified by you alone, and you cease to put out emotional feelers to justify your worth.*** As a confident positive breeds confidence and positivity, you then are aligned to reach your inevitable Highest Good, boasting an unstoppable character. When validation is secure within you, self transforms into a spirit of letting go, trusting, and displaying patience and confidence that the universe will manifest that which you desire.

Commit to high-frequency phrases, boasting words of positivity, power, worthiness, happiness, strength, even vanity — Yes, vanity — like,

I am beautiful, I am love, I'm intelligent, I can, I will prevail in achieving my dreams and see how you attract what you say, believe and feel. Let your spirit be empowered with words of confidence, encouragement and can-do-attitude openly. As your thoughts manifest as words, so will your words manifest as action and action >>> reality. Maybe you overlook or simply do not realise how powerful these statements were;

"Yes We Can — Yes We Can!" From the Obama campaign. And "We are in a fight to Restore the Soul of America" — a statement that elevated to the Honorable or Highest Good of our nation — simply powerful. That followed by an unprecedented win, these words send the right message of Greater Good;

"... my fellow Americans, this is America's day. This is democracy's day. A day of history and hope of renewal and resolve through a crucible for the ages. America has been tested anew and America has risen to the challenge. Today, we celebrate the 'triumph not of a candidate,' but of a cause, the cause of democracy. The people — the will of the people has been heard, and the will of the people has been heeded. We've learned again that democracy is precious, democracy is fragile. At this hour, my friends, democracy has prevailed."[41]

Listen, even "Let's Make America Great Again" is a powerful anthem, but when wrapped in the cloak of deceit, narcissism or arrogance, and negativity leading to widespread disdain for its champion, the power of the anthem is lessened which detracts from all that was accomplished, and the original intent is frustrated irreparably. Stay mindful and positive, then be grateful as goodness, honor, affluence, love, respect and abundance floods your coffers. I can do this and so can you! Yes, we can!

---

[41] Joe Biden's inauguration speech transcript, January 20, 2021
https://www.nytimes.com/2021/01/20/us/politics/biden-inauguration-speech-transcript.html

This is the good that reaches beyond the good of the individual and which claims it's throne of the Creator's Good, referred to in Aristotelian-Thomist philosophy as the Highest Good of humanity where the whole is greater than the [sum of its] part[s]. If, then, each human creature shares in the grace and goodness of the Creator, the unity of the parts would be amazing but never as great as the One, yet, "The greatest created good is the order of the whole of creation. Each creature reflects a different aspect of the Divine goodness as no one creature can represent the Divine goodness as a whole. As St. Thomas Aquinas teaches, «Unity belongs to the idea of goodness… as all things desire good, so do they desire unity; without which they would cease to exist. For a thing so far exists as it is one.» (Ia q103, a3 c) Therefore, since creation is a likeness of a goodness that is essentially one, it follows that the multitude of creatures must be brought together, in some way, so as to imitate the divine unity. The unity that belongs to the multitude of creatures is the unity of order, the harmony that binds them all together."[42]

With this ideology, we can start with ourselves to unite the head and the heart, then repair the unification of family, relationships, communities, and even a nation — the majority anyway. But that is contingent on us being of sound mind and body. We need emotional exfoliation most of all, because unity starts with you, an emotionally healthy you. Emotional Exfoliation is a deep cleanse of the soul, of the heart, of your psyche.

You've listened to me talk about my trauma, now I'd like to help you focus on yours in this moment. Taking the time necessary to grieve from a traumatic event ensures the opportunity to experience unconditional healing. Anything loved and lost needs a time of mourning for a new

---

[42] TheJosias.com, The Good, the Highest Good, and the Common Good, POSTED ON FEBRUARY 3, 2015 BY EDMUND WALDSTEIN, O.CIST.

morning. There is no correct or universal way to move through stages of grief, loss, and healing.

The thing to remember is that one allows him or herself time to move through the pain at their own pace without stagnating. No one should attempt to dictate to another how their grief should look or how long their pain should last. Instead, best practice is continuous encouragement to continue pressing forward, giving you the space to process and feel your feelings. The ability of healing happens to every individual and does not look the same for everyone.

Now it's your turn to implement the **Scribe and Strike Methodology!** So let's do it together. Pause — Go to the Self-check section at the end of this chapter and let your tryouts and emotions flow, strike them immediately, then move quickly to the second task of emitting high vibrational frequencies of self love and positivism. Then return here feeling amazingly powerful!

b. Emotional Barriers

The negative impact of certain situations triggers the individual to block unwanted emotions, establishing barriers possibly to cushion expected pain. Emotional pain is burdensome because it weighs the individual down and prevents the free flow of new emotions to surface.

Holding on to painful emotions creates barriers in one's emotional system.

These emotional barriers are what is referred to as the act of emotional blocking. It is the activity one uses to protect themselves from the weight of what they might feel in stressful situations. Emotional blocks serve as defense mechanisms. These mechanisms act as buffers or barriers to block all or part of an emotion so that one can regain some semblance of normalcy in life. Science and biomedicine is doing just that with advanced blocking vaccines using mRNA and nanotechnology to fight off COVID-19 in an attempt to bring the entire world back to a semblance of normalcy as I write this. The individual uses emotional blocking to allot themselves time to process their emotions gradually.

This eases the stress of having to manage pain they may not feel capable of managing. Mindfulness aids one in managing their emotions properly. Increased mindfulness also increases the individual's capacity to acknowledge, understand, and express their feelings.

These emotional barriers result from sudden traumatic events that have taken place in a person's life. A traumatic event is an event that causes significant and sudden unforeseen stress that threatens one's safety or sense of well-being. If the blockage persists over time, the individual loses their ability to distinguish their emotions from their experiences. Prolonged trauma in the body also interferes with their belief about themselves and the world around them, meaning that the individual has lost the ability to gauge responses because of the emotional barrier.

Emotional blocks occur when the residual energy left from the emotional trauma stays submerged, being re-lived on a subconscious level.[43] Emotional blocks influence difficulty with matters of the heart. When we suppress angry or sad emotions, the flow of positive energy becomes blocked resulting in adverse effects on the individual's total well-being. These blocks live in one's subconscious and have profound influence on behavior and perception. Emotional wounds and trauma live inside the body. Emotions may not presently affect a person, but the body remembers those emotions. The effects of unhealed and unprocessed emotion become cemented in the body's emotional DNA.

---

[43] De Rosa, Wendy. How to overcome emotional blocks with energy healing. https://thriveglobal.com/stories/how-to-overcome-emotional-blocks-with-energy-he aling/.

c. Emotional Healing

When proper grieving and healing periods are honored, one can then learn to confidently release the pain and find new ways to move forward in life. Releasing past pain does not negate the existence of the pain, it promotes healthy living. Sporting a healthy lifestyle does not include carrying the burden of emotional pain.

The absence of healing stunts the mental, emotional, and spiritual growth. If anyone has a desire to become better than they were the day, week, month, or year before, healing must take place. It increases one's ability to have more meaningful experiences in life. Healing creates a deeper connection to self and spirit. Everything in this realm of being is energetic, hence the principle of vibration. Everything is in motion.

We all are energetic beings, and our emotions are vibratory as well. One must exfoliate the negative energy that is preventing the flow of positive emotions to enter. Poor emotional health has negative effects on a person's physical well-being. Whatever hard feelings that are held can be released, cleared, exfoliated and the cycle of healing can be completed.

The process of healing takes time. One does not filter through each phase of healing quickly and should not be expected to. It does not matter the length of time since a traumatic event took place, there is hope for healing for anyone who has experienced life altering trauma. One must take time to learn how to reconnect first with themselves. Then they will be better able to open themselves to the possibility of trusting an honest connection with others.

Only God knows the depth and degree of heartbreak I experienced that morning. The arresting sadness that shadows pieces of my heart are because either I blocked or buried those emotions, and I must find the willingness to trust that God will not fail in helping me to properly grieve and release that sadness. Unconditionally loving myself implies that love is always infinitely available and all that I need to do is learn to tap into that power.

Tapping into the power of the infinite will empower me to love through the muck and mire of my own pain. Even when circumstances are unfavorably murky, love is always possible and will wade its way through. The divine grace of God can change a person's heart effortlessly. Loving myself without limit and practicing patience and grace with myself first wills me to do the same for others.

I have become better able to not overly punish myself if I make mistakes. You can and should do the same. Why? Good question. Because, it's abusive. It's abusive to handle yourself or anyone with anything other than love. For me, learning not to be abusive towards self has been one of the most difficult curriculums to learn. Perhaps you will fair better at this course, but be forewarned, it's much deeper than just academics. The pure science of it is elementary to reverse, the action/reaction principle, as applied to nature. But it's not natural and it boasts a complexity that will require against the grain mentality, emotional exfoliation, prayer, forgiveness, trust and the power of God to get you through.

Many of us beat ourselves up when we falter, constantly rewinding the failure and playing it back in our mind. I have come to know that mistakes do not deem people incompetent, it means they are human. Mistakes do not define the character or integrity of a person. The behavior after the mistake reflects the character of the individual.

Everything in life starts with self. You can only begin to become your best self when first you learn to love self unconditionally. Make the choice not to place any restraint on what is necessary for you to live and be at your fullest capacity. This world deserves the very best of who we are authentically at the core, our center of being, and a regimental approach involving emotional exfoliation can guide us back to a premium, optimal state of wellness at the core.

Operating in ways that dishonor the authenticity of who we all are is detrimental to the well-being of everyone at ground zero. Choose not to detonate a nuclear weapon by dishonoring true heart, for you and your truth reside at ground zero as well. Once we learn, know, and understand the entire center of our being, we can begin to pour from a heart that overflows with the purest most gentle love known to humanity. Operate in and of your highest self governing according to what resides within your soul.

Others will see only the best in us when presenting ourselves in the fullness and light of the divine. That which lives within is what will manifest outwardly.

One very important part of the healing process is to devote attention to what caused the need for healing. Healing is the result of what can potentially be a strenuous process. It is best to first understand the root and stages of pain as it pertains to grief and loss. One must walk through the pain to be freed from it and the detriment it has caused. Losing a loved one or simply losing your way, being shunned is never easy, even though we all know death, risk, fear and human atrocities are an inevitable part of life. No one is ever fully prepared for the downside of life, but we were coded with the DNA to figure it out.

One can try to brace themselves for the unknown, but it's already programmed in your DNA. So when harsh reality collides into your happy-go-lucky fantasy world, the reaction component determines if the brace was properly constructed. Your sense of preparedness eludes you if your defense mechanism doesn't fully deploy, then at 20,000 feet you are thrust into a virtual free-fall because of a malfunctioned parachute. What is programmed into your DNA must be activated precisely at the moment the panic button is triggered because the shock and awe event launches with the element of surprise, so there is no time to think or prepare at that point.

The problem is that we are not rigorously trained as assassins of the shock of traumatic events. Proper assimilation escapes, leaving the individual to go through multiple stages of emotion. Those stages of loss can be universal to most, yet specific to every individual's circumstance.

My single worst experience sequenced stages of grief and loss a bit differently than the experts say: shock and disbelief, sadness and depression, acknowledgment, acceptance, and adaptation. Your reality may be misaligned with what the experts outline as well, and so I will briefly take you through each stage I experienced chronologically.

ii. Stages of Loss

a. Shock and Disbelief

Shock and adrenaline rushed upon me like a thief in the night, unexpectedly. And so, confusion set in with an increased heart-rate and a crippled system of incoherent thought and apprehension. Once the initial shock subsided, disbelief began to overshadow most if not all my emotions. It can be difficult to believe the reality in the making, taking place real-time which seems exaggerated at that given moment. The very first thing most people say upon hearing the news of loss is that it is hard to believe. For me, the experience was surreal, incredible—Not possibly real.

Now that I search the caverns of my mind replaying the events to explain my emotions to you, I have stumbled upon a missing piece of my troubling loss. Mamma did say something earlier that week that could have led up to her misfortune.

All I can remember her saying was, "I need a coke, I need to belch." She thought it was gas that would not move. What she thought was gas, I recall at the emergency room and then into the room we were taken, the doctor who attempted to console me said that she experienced what seemed to be mild heart attacks and then he — the doctor told me and my father she had a massive heart attack and he couldn't bring her back.

Disbelief is a very prominent stage in the loss process, more so than denial. I was not in any way awakened from that nightmare. I kept hoping it was a dream and that I would soon wake up but no denial about her passing. Denial implies that a person has declared something true to be untrue, having not occurred.

It was quite true, and I was aware of that fact, so it was not a question of whether it happened, because I knew it did. I was there. I was the first one to see it. It is more a question of whether I wanted to believe or accept that she was gone forever. I didn't want to believe it. I didn't want to have to face life without my mamma. I just didn't want to be without her. She left me alone to live in this wilderness called life. I know it was not her intent to leave, but knowing that does nothing to lessen the pain of my experience. Up until that point, she was all I knew of this world. I can remember there were parts of me that just wanted to hide and not say anything because I didn't want anyone to think I was crazy. It was hard enough hearing that people thought that I was crazy anyway. There was no need to give anyone a reason to keep thinking about it. But the day never came that I would wake up from that horrible nightmare, so I had to muster up the courage to face the days ahead and continue living without her presence.

b. Sadness and Depression

Sadness isn't far behind the onset of loss's free-fall at terminal velocity. The secondary parachute deploys perfectly well, dangling sadness under the canopy after sustained injury from the ballistic impact of Shock and

Disbelief. During the initial phase of my disbelief, there was a blurred line of sadness. Disbelief and sadness did and, apparently, often does overlap. They blended seamlessly. Because of blurred lines, my disbelief morphed into sadness evoking a plethora of emotions, and the tears from loss preceded the fear of being alone in this world, having lost my protective shield and provider.

The only emotion prevalent in my memory is fear. Fearing the unknown made me sad. Being the only kid in my neighborhood who had experienced that, made me even more sad. Of course, I put on a brave face but on the inside, I was incredibly sad. Interestingly enough though, I didn't want anyone to feel sad or sorry for me, so I didn't talk about it. Life just kind of kept going, and I went right along with it. I could not really expect my friends to do much as we were only thirteen. I am pretty sure they didn't know what to say or do, and neither did I. Even though I have no recollection of them being there, I am grateful that a parent brought them to support me the day we laid mamma to rest. I am told that it was a few of them who rode on the back of a pickup truck to show up for me.

That was indeed special and always makes me smile. I do remember going to view her a few days before the service to give final approval to the funeral home. I remember being there and every time I would look away and look back at her, it seemed that a smile grew on her face. Nobody could tell it was happening but me. I will always believe that was her way of letting me know that she was okay and that I would be okay too. My memory pops in momentarily as I remember having a hard cry at the wake. I remember someone taking me outside but not sure who. I don't remember anything else about that night nor do I remember getting up the next day to go to the funeral. The only thing I remember about the funeral was that they sang my mamma's favorite song, Rough Side of the Mountain. My memory pops back in at the grave-site just before the minister begins committing her body to the ground and I didn't want to go down there, so I stood back at a distance.

It was cloudy that day. My cousin, who later became my best friend walked over to be by my side and I remember telling her, "Please don't come over here crying." I just couldn't handle anymore sadness or tears.

My brain's Memorex™ doesn't play back anything recorded with clarity until events occurring several days later. I don't remember the move or even packing up my things, apparently erased or never permanently recorded because of a chemical imbalance from intense emotions. I guess you could say the Memorex™ cassette of my memory suffered, experiencing similar symptoms and conditions as Alzheimer's. The overwhelming stress of the loss pressed play but not record simultaneously. Just like that, I was at my sister's house, no memory of events in between as the tape's film rolled with no impressions or imprint "real" to reel. Life went on. I imagine the sadness within those days was just too much to bear so I unwound the cassette tape and reel, buried it, and I now cannot recall any of them.

c. Acknowledgment and Acceptance

After the sadness came acknowledgment. Quietly but verbally, the acknowledgment of the experience is necessary. Once the

acknowledgment eased to the forefront, acceptance was soon to follow. As hard as it was, I had to accept my tragic reality recorded, etched in the reel of life. No more hugs, kisses, comforting voice, advice, stories, arguments even, or baked goodies from the bestest. Wow! That's — that's — that doesn't even seem credible.

As the days kept coming, I got better with accepting that that was my new normal. I had to acknowledge that I didn't understand God's plan, but

I had to accept his decree and continue to try and live the best way I knew how.

d. Adaptation

The one phase that seems, in my research, to be colored by omission is adaptation. After loss, loved ones must adjust to the new normal of living with less than the seemingly good or perfect situation they once had. Learning to live without or with a set of less appealing circumstances can be a daunting adjustment to make. It demands one to adopt new ways of being. So, you must be open to adaptation. As stated in Learning and Self-Evolution, adaptation assumes that there is reason to discontinue traveling down the same unfruitful orchard row, rather adjusting to the currency of the immediate environment. There is also no profit or sensibility in picking unripe fruit that has no use. Trained response or behavioral learning moves you from an unproductive state to productivity and wellbeing. We discussed AI and the neural synthesis of human intelligence being the end all using the fundamental forms of adaptation: learning and evolution. AI has a direct correlation to human intelligence because it is derived from and managed by human intelligence. Combining learning and evolution with Artificial Neural Networks says it all.

I am eternally grateful that my sister and her husband sacrificed to keep my life as normal as possible, but I did have to make some adjustments. Because we lived outside of the school district, I had to get to school very early — I mean, so much so that I was always the first kid there. If the bell had not rang for the first homeroom alert, kids would have to go to the cafeteria. But because I got there so early, I would have to sit outside until the doors were unlocked. Yeah, that early.

There was a long cement wall just outside the cafeteria and I would sit there until the janitor would unlock the door for the day. He must have been a godsend, because before long, he started opening the door early so that I would not have to sit outside alone. It was the little things along the way that helped me to adjust. That evolved into me being able to go to a friend's house before and after school. That allotted me time to be with my friends from my neighborhood which helped to keep me grounded and gave me some semblance of normalcy. I would imagine the adjustment was harder for her than it was for me, but somehow, we all made it through to the other side. I am sure that she was not expecting to gain a whole other person to take care of, but she did it without question. I am forever grateful for her selfless act, because she could have rejected me. She didn't have to do that, because I was not her responsibility, not her child; I was her little sister, and I did have a father and a grandmother.

The grace of God carried us through those years. We had good and bad days as any family would, but our willingness to not let tragedy stall us for too long kept us grounded. I cannot for certain say that I was angry at God for mamma's passing, but I was certainly angry about the ordeal. I didn't identify the target of that emotion. I'm not sure why, I just didn't process it. I do know that the essence of who I was and would become changed in that moment she didn't respond when I called her name. I was angry at the situation. I was angry with her for leaving. She was not supposed to leave me. I understand that it was not her choice, but the little girl in me still did not and does not understand that.

iii. The Law of Grace

Grace, in a word, is "free" as in a free gift, derived from the Greek word, charis, meaning divine favor or free gift, and the Hebrew word, chesed, meaning loving kindness. Often associated with mercy, the Greek word, eleos, meaning outward pity or sympathy, they work hand in hand but are not exactly the same. Mercy is viewed as taking pity upon someone and usually given by someone superior to the receiver, and grace is freely given by anyone, peer or otherwise, meaning it's not earned and has no prescribed origin or requirement.

Grace is a natural remedy in healing, and combined with love, it transcends pain and fear. God's grace is supernatural and sufficient for all through divine intervention. His grace is the pinnacle of emotional exfoliation for he grants grace to heal when we are too entangled in webs of woe to free ourselves of the poison feeding the trauma. Likewise, grace is sufficient through practicality. Grace is offered through mercy, compassion, forgiveness and love. When the heart is opened unto unconditional love, it is grace that flows abundantly, overshadowing all else. It is the influence of the spirit which manifests as virtuosity in human behavior.

Just as all of humanity wants and needs God's grace, it must be realised that one must render that same grace to others. Grace is given through compassion and forgiveness. Empathy and unconditional love are qualities that bestow grace. We eliminate ill karmic consequences when we have an attitude and heart that renders grace upon an offender. Spirit negates negative action by dispensing feelings of compassion and forgiveness. The divine energy of grace influences one to have a heart to serve.

The extension of mercy equates to the extension of lending a helping hand to others in need. Divine grace causes one to pray for others. It is spiritual support to those in need. Even in the fumbles of life, grace is given to pardon the wrongs or simply dismiss those that occur even when the intention isn't in the right context. Some might say that grace is given to those who are undeserving. If grace is considered a free gift used in conjunction with mercy which is in-turn an extension of givingness, why would anyone not be deserving of it, you ask?

Now that that's an amazing question for such amazing grace to field. So, hear this O' Israel — None are righteous, no not one. So what does that mean? Simple: no one is deserving of grace because it would defeat the entire purpose and nature of grace. Grace is a gift, a gift given by God, a gift given by a victim, a gift to one who has not earned the worthiness of that very gift, meaning the gift of grace is characteristic of being reserved for and given to the "undeserving." Grace is not envisaged and sanctioned from the recipient's point of view, but the grantor of grace. So just how amazing is this grace? I don't know, you tell me, because I can't put a boundary nor value on it — Grace is amazingly infinite, wouldn't you say? — kind of like it's champion, the Creator.

We are all individuated expressions of God in human form, so why again is there even an idea that someone is not deserving of something that is a part of the whole, the meaning and character of the divine? Now you get it — it just is, and we are sinners, undeserving! Grace is always sufficient, at least it is by God. To some, it does not make sense that God would create us and then not bestow his grace upon us, but we must realise that our sovereign God owes us nothing; no, not even grace, yet He parts with grace and compassion, blessing whom He chooses. That's the God that we serve.

Exodus 33:19 "... I will be gracious to whom I will be gracious, and I will have compassion on whom I will have compassion." (NKJV)

The only hindrance of God's grace would be the denial of his presence and blasphemy of the Holy Spirit. Because of free will, one has the free range to receive the grace of God when he bestows it upon the recipient. It is only when we close ourselves off from God that we don't have the option to receive the blessings of God. Closing oneself off would be disbelief in the power of God's ability to change situations in life. When we don't believe God can do a thing meaningful in our lives, then he probably will not. God has no requisite to prove that he is God.

We put God in a box in our feeble beliefs and then get angry when he doesn't operate inside the little box that we put him in. So if we put God in a box, then how much more appropriate that we should do the very same to our own in relationships of any kind. This is exactly what I experienced.

How can we limit a limitless consciousness? It is impossible. If I had the chance to go back and talk to the little girl inside of me, there are so many things I would want to tell her. She needs to know that it will be ok and that she is divinely covered and that God's grace is sufficient.

Self-check

Scribe and Strike your trauma induced negative thoughts which you cling on to to free yourself from their grip?

_____

_____

_____

_____

_____

_____

_____

Follow up your Scribe and Striking of toxic emotions you with positive thoughts of self praise, hope and joy to vibrate out frequencies of positive promise so that the universe will return to you what you vibrate out.

_____

_____

_____

_____

_____

_____

_____

11 UnKonditional WORDS TO SELF ENCOURAGE

You will revert back after striking. Simply release it, write, and strike again as often as you need to. It's an iterative process of deep emotional exfoliation. Then be sure to speak powerfully about your life!

Alone was what I felt. I was angry and sad and didn't know how to process those feelings. I understood what death was, just not that it could so viciously hit home. My hopes of reversal were obviously futile, yet I had that desire given my umbilical attachment.

~~A little girl should not have to live life without her mother, without the one person who means most to her. I had people around me, but, inside, my heart was racing in sadness, too busy trying to put on a brave face avoiding being called crazy. I had friends who implied that I might be crazy when I express questions about her after death. I wanted to know what she was thinking.~~

~~I had thoughts of her leaving because she didn't want to be my mother anymore. I dreamed that she had moved on, found another family. I just kept wanting and wishing that she would come back. I kept thinking and hoping that one day I was going to wake up from that nightmare and things would go back to being normal. She was supposed to teach me about being a woman.~~

I am determined, I am uplifted, I am on a path of success, and I love me some me.

A Candid Epistle to my Inner Young Self

My Sweet Dee Dee,

I am the part of you that is all grown up now. I have been thinking a lot about you and trying to understand how you feel. Truth is, I don't know what you feel, and having lived your experience, I don't know the level of pain you hold inside. And I apologize up front that I may be a bit long winded, but I have so much I need to share and say to you. I am unapologetic in that I will speak to you as you are a young woman, because you are intelligent enough to understand the words and concepts that I will share with you as you grow. In doing so, I hope that I am able to help you help me to help us.

I want to change the mental image I have of you. You should be laughing and enjoying life in the images of you in my head. And I want to spin your focus from the negative pole to the positive. Because of the trauma you endured, I hesitate with trusting my heart to anyone. I give them everything but myself and I know that it's because of our insecurities. Our hearts suffered through an unspeakable tragedy causing severe wounds of trauma. I think you buried your pain because it hurt too much to endure it.

Please understand, it is okay to keep those feelings buried if it is too prickly to embrace, but if you are ever ready to release them, I will be your agent. I will not abandon you, and I promise to hold your hand until your heart heals and no longer palpitates of aches and fear. I must be honest with you though, your heart will probably always have memory of the hurt you've endured, but as time passes the pain lessens and you will learn to live despite your pain.

You are resilient, and I know that finding mamma was the scariest thing you have ever had to experience, but you need to know that you can and have survived. I know you have not felt safe since that morning, but I am here to protect you. You can trust I will always protect you. I want you to know that you are safe with me.

Because pain is a part of life, there are things that will surely cause you to hurt emotionally. You can trust I will not let you hurt alone. I love and honor your courage unconditionally. You endured the unimaginable and kept standing. I am so proud of you for being that strong, especially at such a young age.

There is something special about you that the world needs to see. You will never have to question my love for you. I know you want to know why our mother's departure too soon, and I am sorry, but I don't have the answer to that question. But the way to ease our pain is help others deal with it.

You can do that, can't you? Use your sensitivity to let them know they will be okay, just like you are and have been. You need to know that God heard your prayer. It was just time for mamma to go. God loves unconditionally. There was nothing you could have done differently, so don't fault yourself for not knowing what to do in that moment.

You don't have to be afraid to talk to God and express how you feel, even if you are angry. God wants you to express how you feel because your feelings are valid. Never let anyone invalidate you or your feelings. I think God wants you to tell him if you are upset or sad.

I want you to try hard to open your heart and let love in. You have a beautiful soul with pure love, and this world needs your kind of love to help it heal. Don't be afraid to love when you have the chance. You are not crazy, nor are you evil because of your experiences. Those people who said those things about you have no idea and are ignorant of how beautiful you truly are.

This world can be a scary place for certain. To have to live your life without the one person who was your whole world is not going to be an easy journey. Be courageous in your fear and be encouraged. It is okay to be angry because your safe space was disrupted, but you can create safety on your own terms. You create your safety by enforcing your boundaries. Boundaries are how you make others aware of how you wish to be treated and respected. They put limits on what you will and will not accept from people.

Standing firm in what you believe is right regardless of what anyone says. Always listen to your own heart. Yes, there will be people who's desire is to hurt you because they themselves are hurting. Just be forewarned that you will allow those people to hurt you under the false pretense that it's ok because you love them. Love is not an excuse to excuse their actions. They are not as well versed in managing their emotions, and sometimes you, the stronger one, will need to fully understand yours and their emotions and figure out the best way to make peace or departure.

The difference between you and them is that you can and will learn positive ways to express your anger rather than weaponizing it to hurt other people. That is what makes you stronger. You are a beautiful person with a beautiful soul, and I want to help you walk into the light of who you were created to be.

Yes, losing mamma hurts, but living life in sadness does more harm than it does good. I am not trying to tell you not to be sad, because there is constant sadness in losing a parent. But you must remember not to let the sadness control how you relate to yourself and others. Be smart with your emotions. Just try to focus on the positive memories of experiences you had with mama. Those beautiful memories will make you smile, quelling the noise level of your sadness. If you can do that, I will benefit as well. Do what you can to manage it and find the happiness you deserve.

You don't need to dim the light within you for other people's light to shine. The light within you is just another way to emit the stuff which paints you uniquely. What I mean by that is that you don't have to make other people feel good about themselves by downplaying the strength of your own personality. You and your feelings matter, so you don't have to hide what you really feel.

I understand that you are angry, but anger has a target and an expensive price tag. Can you tell me who you are angry with, is God your target? Don't be afraid to voice it. Do you know? I will help you figure that out so that we can take it to God in prayer, even if it is God himself you're angry with. While you have these feelings, and it's ok to be angry, keeping it pent up within you is not cheap, and our health will pay the price. So you must learn to release it, just like gas, lol. Be cautious in how you express it as well because it will determine the success of relationships with everyone you meet. Whatever you do, don't become bitter, allowing people an avenue to make you feel as if your heart is hardened which makes you hard to love, because you are love and the light of the divine radiates in everything that you do. You are better than bitter.

People are not always going to support you, so be prepared to support and encourage yourself. You can do and be anything in this world you so desire. Be happy, beautiful one. Mamma wanted you to be happy, the doctor said it, her spirit's growing smile confirmed it, God decreed it, and that settles it. I want you to be happy and at peace, stress-free, without worry. I honor and admire your strength to fight and find a normal life after such an ordeal. You will get through this.

Your sensitivity is a gift. Protect it, and allow no one to change that about you. You don't have to be afraid of falling, thinking that no one will catch you if you do. Please understand, if you ever feel yourself falling, you can trust that I will catch you.

You were taught not to depend on people because they will let you down, and, quite frankly, there are times where I might even make a mistake which causes you disappointment. But I hope you find it in your heart to forgive me if I do. Forgive others too, because the power of healing is in forgiveness. Importantly, you are not an island. In fact, we are not an island, so while trusting and depending on others is like walking a high wire or balanced beam 10 stories off the ground, there will be appropriate situations where relying on others is a part of your success. So, do not alienate yourself, for no man is an island. Just be aware, vet those you must place trust in and tread with caution, step back and a low them the space to be themselves and do what they do to partner with you. For those that do not fit your profile of serenity happiness and success in relationships, romantic, business or friendly, jettison them, for they will profit you nothing but dejection. Sever ties cleanly and quickly, and don't allow bad feelings, bad vibes, and bad blood to flow viscously and fester to the point of hatred, cruelty and tragic loss.

I am a part of you, and I will always hold you close to love your hurt away. I can and will love you past your pain. I can love you amid your traumas. But I would rather love and embrace you in our new home at the corner of Felicity Avenue and Desires of My Heart Street.

Sadness is in your background, and I don't want you to continue to wear that dejection like a shield. I want you to trust me, because when you learn to trust me, I can learn to trust myself. In trust, we will inherit happiness.

*Love**You**Lots,*

Me.

Self-check

If you had the chance, what would you say to your inner child?

_____

_____

_____

_____

_____

_____

_____

_____

_____

_____

_____

_____

_____

12 Final Unkonditional WORDS OF THE ENCOURAGED

One is never fully prepared for the downside of life, but we were coded with the DNA to figure it out.

Whew! I got a lot off of my chest, and I hope you have too. I have faith that this will be a game changer for me. The funny thing about faith and healing faith is that you're either all in or out period. The interesting conundrum of love, respect, sacrifice, and forgiveness in relationships is that most people expect and are looking to receive them unconditionally while holding on to conditions. We use the conditions to justify not reciprocating unconditionally.

Most people have become so engrossed in what benefits themselves that they are not even aware of how to give of anything unconditionally. We have allowed ego to make us selfish with love and respect. In my journey home to myself, I understand the sudden demise of my mother left me with a huge fear of losing people I care about.

That fear caused me to cultivate relationships where I abandoned my own needs for the sake of the relationship. Because I didn't want to feel the pain of loss, I compromised myself just to say I had people who wanted to be in a relationship with me. The irony here is that I ended up losing all of them at some point anyway.

Those losses made me question myself, and I believed something was wrong with me. I could not understand why I would still lose relationships when I had done everything possible to keep them. But those relationships didn't have a foundation of mutual respect, love, or trust. I built those relationships on a need that I provided, and when that provision was no longer available there was no longer a reason to maintain relational ties.

Unconditional love is not the unconditional acceptance of destructive behavior. It is in those moments that we must let go, but that does not mean that the wish for them is anything other than the Highest Good God intended. When a person's presence no longer serves a positive purpose and there is no amicable resolution, then their time in our life must lessen or end.

Gaining clarity brings about new realisation that harmful and abusive relationships end in disaster. Remove the posture of cultivating relationships that don't allow the space one needs to be free to encompass all of who they believe themselves to be.

Never compromise yourself for the benefit of someone else. Accept nothing less than what you desire for the sake of being in a relationship. We should love each other because of who we are and not because of a need to use the weaker as a prop for one's ego. There is no greater pain than to see the misuse of a person who has genuine intentions at heart. One can still love people who dishonor them without allowing them the opportunity to remain close enough to destroy their wonderful spirit. We should never take love for granted.

As spiritual beings, we must serve each other in a capacity of love. I must always exemplify that love and grace for everyone. If I am to operate in the love and light that God has placed within me, then I must always be sure I am a person who lives in the truth of what I speak. When God brings it to my attention that I am not operating in the love he has commanded, I must convict myself and do what is right to serve the Highest Good of myself, and the Greater Good of all.

And as for all of us, recall that one is never fully prepared for the downside of life, but we were coded with the DNA to figure it out.

Self-check

Have you allowed bad behavior of others longer than you should have?

_____

_____

_____

_____

_____

_____

_____

What boundaries have you set in place going forward?

_____

_____

_____

_____

_____

_____

_____

_____

_____

NAMASTE

Bibliography/Citations

1. Trionfo, Victor (Alias), Editor in Chief, 2001

2. Friesen, Garry, ThM, ThD and Maxson, J. Robin, ThM, Decision Making and the Will of God: A Biblical Alternative to the Traditional View, Revised Edition

3. Neural Network Concepts, The Complete Guide to Artificial Neural Networks: Concepts and Models,

https://missinglink.ai/guides/neural-network-concepts/complete-guide-artificial-neural-netw orks

4. Beck, Kevin, DNA vs RNA: What are the Similarities & Differences? (with Diagram), Updated April 23, 2019

https://sciencing.com/dna-vs-rna-what-are-the-similarities-differences-with-diagram-13718 421.html

5. "Adenosine" Merriam-Webster.com Medical Dictionary, Merriam-Webster, https://www.merriam-webster.com/medical/Adenosine. Accessed 3 Feb. 2021.

6. "Adenine." Merriam-Webster.com Medical Dictionary, Merriam-Webster, https://www.merriam-webster.com/medical/Adenosine. Accessed 3 Feb. 2021

7. Beck, Kevin, DNA vs RNA: What are the Similarities & Differences? (with Diagram), Updated April 23, 2019,

https://sciencing.com/dna-vs-rna-what-are-the-similarities-differences-with-diagram-13718 421.html

8. Ibid.

9.   COONEY, ELIZABETH, How nanotechnology helps mRNA Covid-19 vaccines work, DECEMBER 1, 2020 Reprints, BIOTECH, STAT Reports: Nanotechnology in Medicine

https://www.statnews.com/2020/12/01/how-nanotechnology-helps-mrna-covid19-vaccineswork/

10. Ibid.

11. YOUR HEALTH, Understanding mRNA COVID-19 Vaccines, https://www.cdc.gov/coronavirus/2019-ncov/vaccines/different-vaccines/mrna.html

12. Bloomberg vaccine tracker. https://www.bloomberg.com/ https://www.bloomberg.com/graphics/covid-vaccine-tracker-global-distribution/

13. Greene, Robert, 48 Laws of Power, Plan All the Way to the End, Carl von Clausewitz, 1780-1831, pg 237

14. Trionfo, Victor (Alias), Editor in Chief, 2021

15. Greene, Robert, 48 Laws of Power, Plan All the Way to the End, pg 244

16. https://www.discovermagazine.com/the-sciences/einsteins-grand-quest-for-a-unified-theory

17. Neural Network Concepts, The Complete Guide to Artificial Neural Networks: Concepts and Models,

https://missinglink.ai/guides/neural-network-concepts/complete-guide-artificial-neural-netw orks/

18. Daniel Septimus. The Thirteen Principles of Faith. 2002 – 2020.

https://www.myjewishlearning.com/article/the-thirteen-principles-of-faith/

19. Mishneh Torah, Foundational Laws of the Torah, 1.9, https://www.myjewishlearning.com/article/maimonides-rambam/

20. Ibid

21. Silberman, Lou Hackett. Judaism. July 20,1998.

https://www.britannica.com/topic/Judaism/additional-info#history. Encyclopedia Britannica, Inc. June.2020

22. Al-Jaza'iry, Abu Bakr Jabir, Lecturer in the Noble Prophetic Masjid, Volume 1: Minhaj

Al-Muslim, A Book of Creed, Manners, Character, Acts of Worship and other Deeds, First Edition March 2001, Chapter 1, Creed, pg. 19)

23. Ibid, pg 43

24. Ibid, pg 48

25. Ibid, pg 58

26. Ibid, pg 76

27. Ibid, pg 92

28. abuaminaelias.com

29. Roget's Thesaurus (1998) p. 592 and p. 639

30. Trionfo, Victor (Alias), Editor in Chief, Veritable Quandary of Untainted Love

31. The Bitter End Yacht Club in the British Virgin Island's Virgin Gorda, decimated by Hurricane Irma in 2017.

32. Trionfo, Victor (Alias), Editor in Chief, You!niversal You!nique, 2021

33. Wikipedia,
https://en.wikipedia.org/wiki/Color_wheel_theory_of_love,The Color
Wheel theory of love. 2020, accessed February 20, 2021

34. Terrell, Jon. 2012 – 2020. Help with grief, anger, fear, and other
difficult emotions. https://emotional-healing.org/

35. Mary Fairchild. (2019) What does the Bible say about
Forgiveness…https://www.learnreligions.com/what-does-the-bible-say-
about-forgiveness-70 1968

The Free Encyclopedia. Forgiveness. 2020.
https://en.wikipedia.org/wiki/Forgiveness

36. Shaw, George Bernard,
https://quoteinvestigator.com/2014/08/31/illusion/

37. Van Oyen, C. Witvilet. T.E Ludwig and KL Vander Lann, Granting
Forgiveness, or harboring Grudges: Implications for emotions, Physiology
and Health, Psychological Science no. 12 (2001): 117-23.

38. Physical and Emotional Exfoliation for Summer, By Lisa Stewart,
Solia Spa and Peri Skin Care, Skin Inc.,

https://www.skininc.com/treatments/body/Physical-and-Emotional-
Exfoliation-for-Summer571139081.html

39. Dead cell references

1. http://biofuelsdigest.com/nuudigest/2018/01/31/oh-smell-that-
smell- deadsk-in-cells-responsible-for-office-stench/

2. www.newsweek.com/bacteria-feast-dead-human-skin-live-inside-
airconditioners-and-make-our-rooms-796803

40. a b J. Maddox; J. Randi; W. W. Stewart (28 July 1988). ""High-
dilution" experiments a delusion". Nature. 334 (6180): 287–290.

Bibcode:1988Natur.334..287M. doi:10.1038/334287a0. PMID 2455869.

J. Benveniste (28 July 1988). "Dr Jacques Benveniste replies" (PDF). Nature. 334 (6180): 291. Bibcode:1988Natur.334..291B. doi:10.1038/334291a0. Archived from the original on 18 October 2009.

Maddox, J., Randwi, J. & Stewart, W. "High-dilution" experiments a delusion. Nature 334, 287–290 (1988). https://doi.org/10.1038/334287a0

41. Joe Biden's inauguration speech transcript, January 20, 2021https://www.nytimes.com/2021/01/20/us/politics/biden-inauguration-speech-transcript.html

42. TheJosias.com, The Good, the Highest Good, and the Common Good, POSTED ON FEBRUARY 3, 2015 BY EDMUND WALDSTEIN, O.CIST.

43. De Rosa, Wendy. How to overcome emotional blocks with energy healing.

https://thriveglobal.com/stories/how-to-overcome-emotional-blocks-with-energy-healing/.

www.ingramcontent.com/pod-product-compliance
Lightning Source LLC
LaVergne TN
LVHW091249080426
835510LV00007B/188